16.-

About the Author

A career in the telecoms industry in UK and global roles has been paralleled by volunteer activities in the engineering profession culminating in chairmanship of the Council of the Institution of Engineering & Technology (IET) from 2006 to 2008. He is currently a Fellowship and Professional Registration Assessor for the IET.

In the 1950s he saw the Boar Stone at Knocknagael, a few miles from his home in Inverness – the beginning of the life-long "intrigue" of Pictish Stones. He found that a background in engineering encouraged logical analysis and in management encouraged synthesis – helping to make the connections between the Symbols on the Stones and the Mysteries of Mithras.

The author is a Fellow of the Institution of Engineering & Technology, and of the Chartered Management Institute. His research and this discovery are, however, as an "independent researcher".

Dedication

Family members have played a large part in this pursuit. Of special mention are my father (Jim) who maybe knew more about the Pictish Symbol Stones than he let on, my sister (Melody) as initial proof reader, my elder daughter (Tara) who has asked searching questions, my younger daughter (Melody) who seems taken by the symbols and what they might mean – walking with some every day as tattoos – and my wife (Annie) who has supported me over many years of research and disappearing to the study!

Norman J. Penny

Pictish-Mithraism, the Religious Purpose of the Pictish Symbol Stones

Copyright © Norman J. Penny (2017)

The right of Norman J. Penny to be identified as author of this work has been asserted by him in accordance with section 77 and 78 of the Copyright, Designs and Patents Act 1988.

All rights reserved. No part of this publication may be reproduced, stored in a retrieval system, or transmitted in any form or by any means, electronic, mechanical, photocopying, recording, or otherwise, without the prior permission of the publishers.

Any person who commits any unauthorized act in relation to this publication may be liable to criminal prosecution and civil claims for damages.

A CIP catalogue record for this title is available from the British Library.

ISBN 9781786290236 (Paperback)
ISBN 9781786290243 (Hardback)
ISBN 9781786290250 (eBook)
www.austinmacauley.com

First Published (2017)
Austin Macauley Publishers Ltd.
25 Canada Square
Canary Wharf
London
E14 5LQ

Acknowledgements

The following books and websites, and their constituent references, have been a learning resource and helped provoke thoughts culminating in the overall discovery of Pictish-Mithraism®. The author attests, however, that the interpretations and rationales leading up to them are wholly his own and have not been plagiarised.

Pictish:
Origins of Pictish Symbolism – James Carnegie Southesk, 1893.
The Early Christian Monuments of Scotland – Allen & Anderson, 1903.
The Origin Centre of the Pictish Symbol Stones (Proc FSA(Scot)) – Isabel Henderson, 1957-58.
Scotland Before History – Stuart Piggott, 1982.
Pictish & Norse Finds from the Brough of Birsay – C L Curle, 1982.
The date and origin of Pictish symbols (Proc Soc Antiq Scot) – L Laing & J Laing, 1984.
The Pictish Guide – Elizabeth Sutherland, 1997.
Picts and Ancient Britons – Paul Dunbavin – 1998.
A Wee Guide to the Picts – Duncan Jones, 1998.
The Picts and their Symbols – W A Cummins, 1999.
The Picts and the Scots – L & J Laing, 2004.
Warlords and Holy Men – Alfred P Smyth – 2005.
Roman Scotland – David Breeze – 2006.

Beyond the edge of the empire – Caledonians, Picts & Romans – Fraser Hunter, 2007.
The Picts – Tim Clarkson, 2008.
The Pictish Symbol Stones of Scotland – Iain Fraser for RCHAMS, 2008.
From Caledonia to Pictland; Scotland to 795 – James E Fraser, 2009.

Mithraic:
The Mysteries of Mithra – Franz Cumont, 1903.
Mithras, the Secret God – M J Vermaseren, 1963.
The Roman Art Treasures from the Temple of Mithras – J M C Toynbee, 1986.
The Origins of the Mithraic Mysteries – David Ulansey, 1989.
The Roman Cult of Mithras – Manfred Clauss – 2000.
The Mysteries of Mithras – Payam Nabarz, 2005.
The Religion of the Mithras Cult in the Roman Empire – Roger Beck, 2006.
Gods with Thunderbolts – Guy de la Bédoyère, 2007.
From Cyrus to Alexander: A History of the Persian Empire – Pierre Briant.

Web sites:
http://www.twmuseums.org.uk/archive/mithras/intro.htm
http://www.roman-britain.org/places/brocolitia.htm
http://www.ostia-antica.org/dict/34.htm
http://en.wikipedia.org/wiki/London_Mithraeum

PICTISH SYMBOL STONES – WHY SO INTRIGUING?

1 THE PICTISH SYMBOL / MITHRAS CONNECTION

2 PICT, PICTLAND, PICTISH – MEANINGS

3 MITRA, MITHRA, MITHRAS – WHO THEY WERE

4 TEMPLES OF MITHRAS – PURSUING ROMAN MITHRAISM

5 CARVINGS ON THE STONES – INITIAL RESEARCH AND ANALYSIS

6 MITHRAIC SYMBOLS IDENTIFIED AND DECODED

7 STONES & DISTANT VIEWS – THE "OPEN AIR" MITHRAEUM

8 THE START OF PICTISH-MITHRAISM – WHO, WHEN AND WHERE?

9 CHANGES IN BELIEFS – STONE USAGE, TIMELINES & TRANSITIONS

10 THE OVERALL PICTISH-MITHRAISM® DISCOVERY

APPENDIX 1 PICTISH SYMBOL STONES – CASE STUDIES

APPENDIX 2 EXAMPLES OF SYMBOL DESIGNS

PICTISH SYMBOL STONES
WHY SO INTRIGUING?

Over 1500 years ago these enigmatic structures appeared predominantly in the north east of what, more recently, has become Scotland. Sometimes they can be confused with the wide array of other standing stones, megaliths, circles and dolmens that do not display symbols.

They are called "Pictish" but who erected them?

Why is there a gap between the naming of the "Picts" by the Roman invaders around the late 3rd Century CE and the generally suggested dates for the erection of the stones? Or are previous estimates incorrect?

Did the existing population erect the stones – or was it incomers?

Who had the skills to carve the stones; and why onto a material that has endured so long? Was this choice of material deliberate?

What do the symbols mean – assuming they do have a specific purpose and give a particular message? Were they for worship, boundary markers, burial indicators, commemorative of specific events, used to educate – or maybe just decorative?

Are the stones located in significant locations?

Why did the symbols on the seemingly older stones carry forward to the newer ones with Christian crosses?

The author's quest was to seek a definitive explanation for the origin and purpose of these stones and what the symbols represent. The result is a significant discovery.

1
THE PICTISH SYMBOL / MITHRAS CONNECTION

Investigations
Wondering if the geometric Pictish Symbols could be some form of structured language led the author, many times, to the British Museum, London, looking at tablets, monuments and cylinder seals with pictographs developing into cuneiform. This early form of recording information (numbers and words) can be seen on carved stone panels from the Assyrian cities of Nimrud and Nineveh.

Clay cuneiform brick; off the outer face of the ziggurat at Nimrud. Licensed image courtesy of British Museum.

Carvings on Assyrian panels prompted the thought that understanding the symbols could be in interpreting the shapes individually and that a language was not being represented.

Nothing was quite like the shapes on the symbol stones until some of the carved images on the large polished stones from Sippar, Mesopotamia (known as kudurrus) were seen to have some similarities such as crescent, bull-like figures, fantastic beasts etc. These kudurrus, erected between the 16th and 12th century BCE, recorded, for example, land transactions and seemingly acted as boundary markers.

Kudurru, Babylonian boundary stone. Licensed image courtesy of the British Museum.

This prompted the question – could the Pictish Symbol Stones be boundary markers? However, the only stone that does have the kudurru style is Logie Elphinstone 2.

Realisation

A chance visit to the Museum of London and its collection of statuary from the third century, CE Walbrook Mithraeum, was the first time the author saw an example of the Tauroctony and its embellishments. The Tauroctony is the real or symbolic slaying of the bull by Mithras – a standard feature of a Mithraeum. This example is full of associated iconography such as a dog, serpent and scorpion with the central scene surrounded by a broad circle enclosing the signs of the zodiac.

Walbrook Tauroctony, London.
Licensed image courtesy of the Museum of London.

Mithras is accompanied by his supporters (to his right and left) – the torchbearers, Cautes and Cautopates. Cautes holds his torch up representing sunrise and the spring equinox. Cautopates holds his torch down representing sunset and the autumn equinox. Deeper investigation into the Mysteries of Mithras shows these torchbearers represent a spiritual meaning – a significant aspect being the travel of the soul on birth and at death. Extensive reading of texts and websites regarding Mithraism – both the original Persian, and the Roman version – surfaced spiritual aspects of the belief and an understanding of the physical and symbolic construction of Mithraea.

Sketching the shapes of the Z-Rod and Double Disc Pictish Symbol the author could see how the horizontal lines of the so-called Z could be the torches of Cautes and Cautopates, with the angled line perhaps being a link to Mithras.

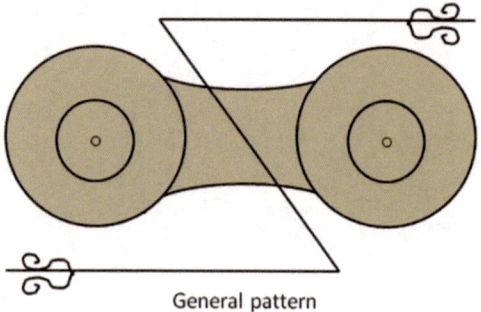

General pattern

A Mithraic belief is that the soul on death travels from Earth, via the planets to the celestial sphere – the discs typically have a central dot (or very small circle) then two concentric circles; these equate to the Earth, planets and celestial sphere.

Delving into the detail of the Roman version of Mithraism enabled several other symbols to be readily interpreted in a Mithraic context.

With the travel of the soul on birth and death it was apparent that the V of the V-Rod is two arrows and the Crescent is a representation of the view to heaven.

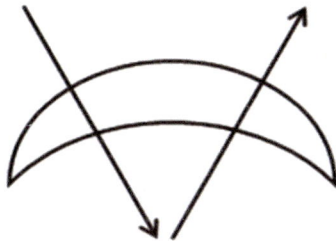

Looking at Mithraic statuary in the Great North Museum in Newcastle it was fairly straightforward to see that the birth of Mithras from the rock can be recognised in the Mirror Case Symbol.

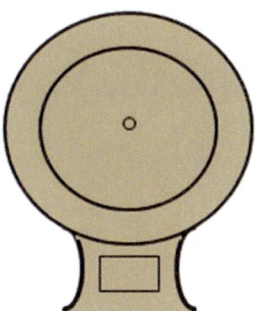

This was an encouraging start – the individual shapes of the symbols did contain a coding.

Detailed research into the origins of writing, looking at and contemplating shapes and researching Mithraism coupled with seeing the Mithraic statuary in the Museum of London was rewarded – it led to the realisation that there is indeed a Pictish Symbol / Mithras connection.

A working title of "Pictish-Mithraism" seemed appropriate – later to be the name of the overall discovery.

2
PICT, PICTLAND, PICTISH MEANINGS

It is useful to draw a brief distinction between these words. Several relevant texts are mentioned in the Acknowledgements.

"Pict" is a label given apparently by Roman invaders in the 3rd century CE to the people who lived, broadly, in what is now known as the North East of Scotland. It is uncertain whether these "locals" gave themselves a particular name, whether they were a single "people" or were a conglomerate of communities. Their geographic origin is uncertain. What is certain is that no-one would have been living in the north of Scotland until about 11,500 years ago – once the ice had substantially cleared. The effects of glaciation would have rendered the inland areas inhospitable to settlers but the coastal areas had the attributes for sustenance – land to cultivate, material for fire for warmth, rivers and seas to fish, animals to hunt for food and clothing, dwelling opportunities (caves, woodland and trees for construction). They were accessible across water, along coastal stretches and, in early (just post-glaciation) settlement times, via land bridges to other parts of what we now call mainland Europe. So descriptors such as indigenous are limited – they may have been original inhabitants of the geographic area but, unlike a non-glaciated area, their start point is a lot later. They most definitely came from somewhere else.

"Pictland" is the term generally used in referring to the geographical location where the Picts lived; mainly the area we now call North East Scotland but varying in size over time to other parts of Scotland – depending on acquired and enforced boundary changes. The map opposite is a snapshot of what seemingly comprised "Pictland" around about 600CE.

"Pictish" can be the adjectival or possessive version of "Pict". It can be used as Pictish person, Pictish place, Pictish time period or era, Pictish country, Pictish Symbol Stones, Pictish xxx etc.

It may be wrong to assume that the only people living in Pictland when the stones started to be created were the supposedly "indigenous" population. This is where the terms "Pictish Standing Stones" and "Pictish Symbol Stones" can be misleading as it tends to suggest the stones were put up by the Picts – this may not be the case and is explored later.

3
MITRA, MITHRA, MITHRAS - WHO THEY WERE

As the intent from the author's research was to see if there is a connection between some form of Mithraism and the symbol stones, a short "Who's Who" is offered to understand the chronology and locations of Mitra, Mithra and Mithras. Several relevant texts are mentioned in the Acknowledgements. This picture is a bust of Mithras as he would have been considered in the time of the Roman Empire; complete with his trade-mark Phrygian cap.

Mithras Bust. Licensed image courtesy of Museum of London.

The geographical and chronological origins are Mithra (a Persian God), Mitra (an Indian God within the pantheon of Vedic Hinduism) and Mithras (the Graeco-Roman version that was followed about the time of the Roman presence in what is now called Britain and across continental Europe and North Africa). This latter belief is familiarly referred to as Roman Mithraism and became a cult following during the time of the expansion of the Roman Empire. It was based on the previous Persian version and was practised across the empire, being particularly popular within the army. Roman Mithraism started to decline with Christianity becoming the "state" religion in the 4th century CE but may have survived in modified form into, at least, the immediate post-Roman period.

Information from a number of sources suggests an approximate timeline:

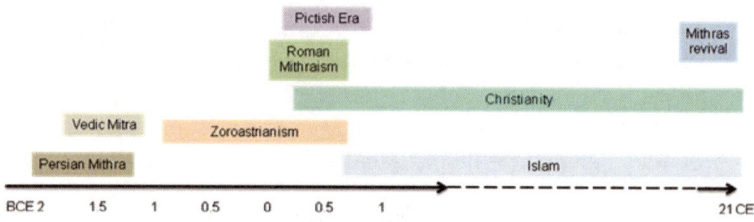

Mithra was deemed the son of Ahura-Mazda, the divine god of the heavens. The original Persian Mithra worship branched out into India where Mithra was known as Mitra. Mithras was based on Mithra but was elevated from a son of God to God himself. Also he has been depicted as Kronos (personification of infinite time) or as the light conquering the darkness. In the bull slaying (Tauroctony) statues associated with Mithraism, Mithras is shown as young, fresh-faced and with no specific racial or birth place identity.

Central to Roman Mithraism is the god called Mithras (Sol Invictus – the Invincible Sun) who had the power to rotate the entire universe. This power was ascribed to him from the discovery by Hipparchus (a Greek astronomer living in the 2nd century BCE) of the precession of the equinoxes whereby the earth has a slight wobble on its axis.

In a polytheistic age the god who could affect this was a powerful god indeed!

The "Mysteries of Mithras" are indelibly linked to the astronomy and astrology as understood and in use at the time. The Earth was considered to be at the centre of the universe with the planets rotating around the Earth in one direction and the firmament (celestial sphere) rotating in the opposite direction. What we nowadays call planets and were known at the time were Jupiter, Mars, Venus, Mercury and Saturn. In addition, the Sun and Moon were, then, considered to be planets.

It must be remembered that the position of constellations relative to Earth in our timeframe (early 21st century) is not necessarily the same as in Roman Empire times; nor, according to David Ulansey, was the position in the early part of the first millennium CE relevant to reading constellations in the context of the Mysteries of Mithras. Allowing for apparent constellation locations for a specific Tauroctony alignment (Mithras killing the bull) involving the constellation Taurus, the significant timeframe is 2000 years before Roman Mithraism i.e. what the sky looked like about 4000 years ago. This is very important to understanding the relative positions of several constellations such that the Tauroctony occurred at a particular time of the year and has in its component constellations both the bull (Taurus) and Mithras (seen as Perseus above Taurus). So, for the Tauroctony to occur at the spring equinox the astronomical and astrological alignments need to apply to the so-called Age of Taurus (we currently are in the Age of Pisces). Texts on Mithraism are referred to in the Acknowledgements.

Mithras is shown in the Tauroctony with a figure on either side – often referred to as his companions. Taking the Walbrook, London example, looking towards the

Tauroctony to the viewers left is Cautes (representing the morning star and spring equinox) and to the right Cautopates (representing the evening star and autumn equinox). Relative to Mithras, Cautes is on his right and Cautopates on his left. These figures are key when decoding the Pictish Symbol Stones.

The number "7" features in Mithraism in several aspects. There were (as known at the time) 7 planets. There were 7 steps as the progression grades in Mithraism; each of these 7 grades has an associated planet. The Plough has 7 stars – it is the Bear which moves and turns the heavens around.

Coupled with a hierarchy of initiation with associated symbolism, a complex interaction between a "hold" over initiates and their progressively gaining more understanding of what the Mysteries were must have enticed and retained membership.

4

TEMPLES OF MITHRAS – PURSUING ROMAN MITHRAISM

The Temple – Mithraeum – was the indoor meeting place for pursuing the Mysteries of Mithras. Remains of Mithraea (plural of Mithraeum) can be seen across many parts of the early first millennium CE Roman Empire – several websites are referenced in the Acknowledgments. Locations such as Mackwiller, Alsace, France; Aquincum, Near Budapest, Hungary; Caernarfon, Gwynedd, Wales; Carrowburgh (Brocolitia), Northumberland, England; Duino, Trieste, Italy; Fertorakos, Hungary; Walbrook, London, England; Ostia Antica, near Rome, Italy; Rudchester (Vindobala), Northumberland, England and Savaria, Szombathely, Hungary can be visited but in addition, other Mithraea are under current churches and many Mithraic altars and statues are in museums.

The Mithraeum would have been suitably laid out and decorated with statues and paintings to enable the followers to gather, to worship, to be talked through (and prospectively walked through) the iconography to understand the Mysteries of Mithras and to progress through the Grades. From remains particularly in Italy, Germany and England there is evidence of specific designs and a regard for compass orientation which has huge significance when considering the relationship of the Mysteries with astrological and astronomical aspects. These were temples – places of spiritual devotion and for instruction. The

Mithraeum was created and constructed as a "virtual universe".

The temples generally were underground or partially underground, sometimes beneath other buildings. Some have also been in caves. For the built temples the structure can be likened to a cave (of significance as Mithras was said to have been born from rock in a cave) but also a model of the macrocosm. Having a semi-circular vertical profile, the typical built structure then also became cave-like. On either side of the long centre line of the Mithraeum (they were rectangular) there were benches and at one end the iconography of the Tauroctony – the bull slaying by Mithras.

Being enclosed, temples were private but something must have enticed people to want to understand the Mysteries; nothing external is apparent from excavations so far – this suggests word of mouth. A detail in several of these temples is niches for statues speculatively for Cautes & Cautopates (Mithras's companions) and other gods.

Mithraea may not just be the plural of Mithraeum – perhaps there was some significance where several are located near one another. By challenging the description above, which tends to suggest a standard Mithraeum, could some have been grouped by location, each serving a differing but complementary purpose? Could there be a hierarchical structure to Mithraea in a particular location (explaining, for example, the high number in Ostia, Italy) – like Christian churches and their relationship with cathedrals? Maybe not all Mithraea catered for all grades?

The Mithraeum at Carrawburgh, Hadrian's Wall, Northumberland (photo – the author).

The House of the Mithraeum of the Painted Walls, Ostia, Italy (image courtesy of Jan Theo Bakker).

*The Mithraeum of the Seven Gates, Ostia, Italy.
Attributed to www.ostia-antica.org*

The London Mithraeum (Walbrook) was discovered in the 1950s with the temple foundations being moved wholesale to a nearby location. The artefacts are in the Museum of London. The statues are collectively dated as being carved between 130 and 200 CE in the Hadrianic (117 to 138) and Antonine (138 to 192) periods. When found, sculptures had been buried in and near the temple. Coin and pottery evidence suggests 240 to 250 for the building of the temple, with the temple in use until 350 with the monuments being buried around 320 to 330.

Some Walbrook statuary is made from imported materials (typically Carrara marble) carved to a high standard. Other material is local to the UK (typically limestone probably from the Cotswolds area) and is more roughly carved. The time lag between the carving of, for example, the Carrara marble statuary and their appearance in the Walbrook Mithraeum suggests these items had previous use, were carved in Italy and imported for use in the temple. The "relief of Mithras Tauroctonos" seems to have been produced specifically for the Walbrook Mithraeum maybe as late as during the first half of the third century. This date is also suggested for the locally produced items made, arguably, specifically for Walbrook.

Beyond Britannia, several Mithraea (from a number of sources) have known or estimated construction dates, such as these:

Dura-Eoropos, Syria has an initial date of 168, a rebuild of 210 and extension of 240; a tablet of 210 offers salutation to Septimius Severus, Caracalla and Geta.

It is speculated that the Caesarea Maritimia Mithraeum in the Roman province of Syria Palestina was built toward the end of the 1st Century.

Several statues (including Cautes, Cautopates and Aion) are in the Louvre, Paris from the Sidon, Syria Mithraeum built in the 2nd century.

Ptuj, Slovenia is mid-2nd Century.

A Mithraeum was built in Bordeaux, France around the end of the 2nd and beginning of the 3rd Century.

The Friedburg, Germany example is dated to the late 2nd or early 3rd Century, as is pottery found within the temple at Mundelsheim, Germany.

Fertorakos Mithraeum in Austria was constructed by soldiers from the Carnuntum legion at the beginning of the 3rd Century.

The Mitreo delle Pareti Dipinte, Ostia, Italy dates to the second half of the 2nd century as does the Mitreo degli Animali and the Mitreo delle Sette Sfere. The Mitreo delle terme di Mitra dates to the first half of the 3rd century. The Mithraeum of the Snakes, also at Ostia, dates to the first half of the 2nd century.

Another Ostia temple – Mitreo Aldobrandini – dates to the end of the 2nd century.

Dating from the beginning of the 2nd century is the Mitreo di Santa Maria Capua Vetere, Campania, Italy.

The second half of the 3rd century is the date given to Mitreo del Circo Massimo in Rome and Mitreo di Felicissimus at Ostia. There are many more Mithraea in and near Rome and nearby coastal areas – especially Ostia. In fact, there are 73 monuments / temples in Italy listed at www.mithraeum.eu

At Merida, Spain, a Mithraeum existed about 155; Mithraic monuments have been found at several sites in Spain dating from the first half of the 2nd century.

The Mitreo de Lugo, Galicia is dated to the early 3rd century – Lugo's altar is dated to 211 to 217 mentioning Mithras and also the VII Gemina Legion.

Near Cordoba is the Mithraeum at Puenti Genil dating from the middle of the 2nd century to the beginning of the 3rd.

The Mitreo dels Munts, Tarragona dates to the 2nd century.

In 1933 at Martigny, Switzerland a Mithraeum built 1750 years earlier was discovered and is preserved in the basement of newly built apartments.

The earliest dates for Mithraeum construction in Britannia are in the early 3rd century i.e. from 200. Beyond

Britannia they are earlier, ranging from the beginning of the 2nd to the second half of the 3rd i.e. between 100 and 299 but generally the first half of the 3rd – the early 200s.

Based on time period and location, any of the Mithraea mentioned above could have been the direct or indirect source of knowledge of the Mysteries of Mithras as practised in Britannia – and could have provided the structural design and layout for an indoor Mithraeum in Britannia. The nearest examples of Mithraea to NE Scotland (the Pictland area we are considering) are by Hadrian's Wall such as Rudchester (Vindobala) and Carrawburgh (Brocolitia).

Before and after gaining entry to a Mithraeum, cult followers would have been impacted by three key aspects – the initial Enticement, the Tauroctony and the Initiation Grades.

Enticement

Roman Mithraism was a mystery cult with the teaching, initiation, religion, astronomy and astrology being well concealed. Its buildings were less easy to hide but entry was restricted. None of this would have encouraged involvement – quite the opposite – but for the cult to exist potential new members needed to know something about it to want to become involved. There arguably needed to be some form of enticement – at minimum giving a taster, at best giving a realisation of a unique selling point such as a spiritual home for life. Perhaps handed down knowledge (from an established initiate) or more general public knowledge of what the cult might offer may have attracted a new member. An expectation that certain groups could or should become members could also have been a draw – for example the cult was especially popular within the military. The hope of a hereafter could have been an enticement – a particular attraction to military personnel, often faced with a shorter than usual life expectancy. None of these is shown as a statue or symbol as such but presumably was passed on by word of mouth. The physical presence of a Mithraeum (with a supposition of what it might contain or what those contents might represent) could have been the nearest there was to visible enticement.

Tauroctony

This "bull-slaying" scene (real or symbolic) was central to (and in) the design of a Mithraeum and positioned to clearly be seen by those in the building – it was not physically hidden but interpretation would have required guidance. The contents always featured the cloaked, Phrygian capped Mithras stabbing the bull with, variously, his companions – Cautes & Cautopates, snake, dog, scorpion, cup, sun, moon, zodiac, representation of the four winds, stars on Mithras' cloak, ears of corn and other carvings.

Tauroctony relief – Neuenheim near Heidelberg
Attributed to www.mithraeum.eu

These grades or rites and associated planets and symbols can clearly be seen in Mithraea in Ostia, Italy. In summary they are:

Grade; Associated Planet; Symbols

1 Corax (raven); Mercury; raven, caduceus, small beaker

2 Nymphus (male bride); Venus; oil lamp, diadem, torch, veil, mirror, bee.

3 Miles (soldier); Mars; lance, helmet, soldier's bag.

4 Leo (lion); Jupiter; fire shovel, rattle, thunderbolt, honey.

5 Perses (Persian); Moon; harpe (curved sword), Persian dagger, sickle, scythe, crescent moon with star, honey.

6 Heliodromus (courier of the Sun); Sun; torch, 7-rayed crown, whip

7 Pater (Father); Saturn; libation bowl, sickle of Saturn, staff and ring, Phrygian cap.

The belief was that at birth an individual's soul came from beyond the celestial sphere and at death travelled back, via the planets. A complete ladder can be considered to start from a base of "0" rising in 7steps (the Mithraic Grades) to the eighth – the celestial sphere, the Milky Way – then through it to Heaven, the home of the soul. All told, therefore, from an Earthly perspective there are ten levels from "enticement" at "0" to "soul return" at "9".

Each object seen in a typical Tauroctony statue can be associated with a skyward view element (planet, constellation etc.).

Tauroctony component with corresponding item in a skywards view:

Cave – the Universe; Sol – Sun; Luna – Moon; Cautes & Cautopates – Gemini; Bull – Taurus; Lion – Leo; Dog –

Canis Minor, Canis Major; Scorpion – Scorpius; Snake – Draco, Hydra – Serpens; Raven – Corvus; Wheat Ear – Spica; Cup – Crater.

5
CARVINGS ON THE STONES – INITIAL RESEARCH AND ANALYSIS

Having made the link between the Pictish Symbol Stones and the Mysteries of Mithras, a significant task has been to research, investigate, record, categorise and analyse all the carvings. Two groupings resulted – those which portray a Mithraic meaning and those which are non-Mithraic objects.

The consistent feature of the carvings that have been discovered to have a Mithraic connection is that they do not have an independent meaning in themselves but can be regarded as representing or standing for something else. They need interpretation – this is not unusual for religious iconography. An added complication in decoding the symbols is that they have been allocated names that are purely descriptive of their shapes. For example, the most numerous carving is the so-called V-Rod and Crescent – an apt description for what the carving appears to be but not putting it into any type of context. Arguably helpful at the time when these names were given, but making the task of decoding more difficult due to this popularly accepted and generally unchallenged labelling.

Key stages of the task were:
Investigating where else there might be designs similar to the non-Christian ones on the Pictish Symbol Stones. Nowhere!

Creating a structure for sorting, recording and analysing the researched material. Every carving is called an object, several objects can be placed in an object category, specific patterns and designs emerged.

Looking at every object, identifying Mithraic symbolism, describing it and then decoding the designs in the context of Mithraic meanings. Design examples are in Appendix 2.

Identifying and describing the non-Mithraic carvings, then associating them with changes in beliefs. See website.

To avoid creating a new and potentially confusing terminology, the names of objects used are those popularly found in Pictish Symbol Stone books and other relevant texts and web-sites. Also, the "Class" categorisation formulated by Allen and Anderson is used but with the addition of functionality so that Class 1 are the initial, or early, stones with Pictish-Mithraism symbols, later Class 2 are in the "transition" between Pictish-Mithraism and Christianity and Class 3 are not "symbol stones" as such, having clearly Christian carvings only.

The stones contain carved objects which are either symbols without immediately clear meaning or items which on the surface may require no interpretation. In reality if there are "secrets" which obscure or protect "mysteries" then every symbol and other item will have a meaning, possibly several, and so require interpretation. Some of the shapes might be thought of as symbols but could be embellishments added, perhaps, at the discretion of the carver or, simply, errors. Some bear resemblance to tamgas (Central Asian markings used to identify property or cattle and also with wider use to represent birds and other meanings) but none so far researched has fitted. Looking at Scandinavian symbols, some similarities with Pictish carvings can be found but not with a strong correlation. Often the stones are described as "unique" bearing no resemblance to symbols or marks or depictions seen anywhere else but this can be a way of dismissing further investigation. Overall they surely must evoke something.

A few examples of the crescent shape seen on Pictish Stones can be seen on Roman carvings – some taken from around Hadrian's Wall are now in the Great North Museum, Newcastle, also at the Corbridge Museum and from Bridgeness, between South Queensferry and Grangemouth, now in the National Museum of Scotland (NMS), Edinburgh.

Bridgeness Slab. Licensed image courtesy of National Museums of Scotland.

The Cappuck Roman carving (now in NMS and originally near Jedburgh) has a Crescent shape and also has a boar – not dissimilar to the Knocknagael Stone (in the foyer of the Highland Council, Inverness). The boar is the symbol of the Roman Twentieth Legion, further prompting a Roman connection.

Corbridge Stone. Photograph – author, with kind permission of English Heritage.

The inscription on this stone at Corbridge, Hadrian's Wall, translates as, "To the Unconquered Sun God a detachment of the 6th Legion Victrix Pia Fidelis set this up under the charge of Sextus Calpurnius Agricola the emperor's propraetorian legate". Note: the "Unconquered Sun God" is Mithras.

The reason for mentioning these stones is that they have crescent shaped objects which, apart from a few examples of mirror-like objects on Roman altars, are the only items the author has seen where there is a shape with resemblance to any on Pictish Stones, notably in the so-called V-Rod & Crescent and Mirror and Comb. This further reinforces the uniqueness of the objects on the Pictish Stones and the lack of picking up styling cues from anywhere.

In decoding the symbols on the stones there is always a need to consider context. The greatest over-riding difference between Pictish and other Mithraic symbolism is that, almost exclusively, the Pictish Symbols are outdoors. Hence it might be deduced that the seeming lack of Tauroctony symbolism is due to the fact that the "bull killing" does not need to be carved – it can be seen in the night sky (Perseus representing Mithras over Taurus the bull). Alternatively, maybe the evolved version of Roman Mithraism either did not include the Tauroctony or hid it in some highly coded objects.

A focus is retained in this publication on standing stones specifically. Carvings not on stones have not been included i.e. Trusty's Hill rock, East Wemyss (Dysart) & Covesea caves and Clashach cove. Some of the shapes seen in these caves can be seen on the stones, often very stylised, and are mixed with other carvings. Carvings that appear to be later copies have also been excluded e.g. the Dunnicaer crescent on triangle and two circles with dots.

In seeking Mithraic elements in symbols on Pictish Stones it would be reasonable to expect to find, obscured or otherwise, shapes that relate to Roman Mithraism, perhaps the Mithraea themselves, such as these:

Statues of Cautes and Cautopates (companions of Mithras) – from Housesteads Mithraeum (photograph – author, with kind permission of the National Trust)

Mithras being born from the Cosmic Egg (stone from Housesteads Mithraeum). Photograph – author, with kind permission of the Society of Antiquaries of Newcastle upon Tyne collection, Great North Museum: Hancock.

As well as physical objects, coded Mithraic representations of beliefs, such as the travel of the soul on birth and death, were expected to be found. Gaining a wide knowledge and understanding of the principles of Roman Mithraism was necessary.

There is a range of carved objects on the stones – "coded symbols", representations of birds, animals, people etc. and readily discernible items such as crosses. An analysis of the most numerous follows. The focus is then on those with a Mithraic context.

ANALYSIS – SYMBOL STONE OBJECTS WITH 10 OR MORE OCCURRENCES

26 objects (each of which has 10 or more occurrences) account for 75% of all carvings on the symbol stones.

Object	Occurrences	Percent of Total
V-rod & Crescent	90	9.85
Mirror	62	6.78
Latin / Christian Cross	58	6.35
Z-rod & Double Disc	56	6.13
"Pictish beast"	51	5.58
Comb	40	4.38
Beast with exaggerated claws	38	4.16
Interlaced animals with Cross	36	3.94
Mirror case	19	2.08
Double disc alone	18	1.97

Horseshoe / arch	18	1.97
Salmon	18	1.97
On horseback / horseman	17	1.86
Hunting	17	1.86
Rectangle (decorated)	16	1.75
Eagle	16	1.75
Triple disc	15	1.64
Linear Ogham	15	1.64
Z-rod & Serpent	11	1.20
Z-rod & Notched Rectangle	11	1.20
Tuning fork	11	1.20
Hippocamp	11	1.20
Serpent alone	10	1.09
Flower	10	1.09
Angel	10	1.09
Dog	10	1.09

6
MITHRAIC SYMBOLS IDENTIFIED AND DECODED

The coding has been so successful that not only has the meaning of the individual carvings on the Pictish Symbol Stones been hidden but so also has their collective purpose. Identifying the shapes of the carvings in the context of a form of Mithraism practiced in Pictland over 1500 years ago has enabled the Pictish-Mithraism Discovery.

Nine key symbols have been discovered that have Mithraic contexts. The first five listed here can particularly be used to describe the principles of Mithraic beliefs– V-Rod & Crescent, Mirror, Z-Rod & Double Disc, Pictish Beast, Comb, Snake/Serpent, Mirror Case, Double Disc and Triple Disc. A further three symbols represent the structure and layout of temples used in Roman Mithraism – Horseshoe/Arch, Notched Rectangle and Tuning Fork. One further carving has design elements seen in other symbols but has not yet been decoded – Decorated Rectangle.

Twelve of these objects (all except the Pictish Beast) have been drawn by the author in PowerPoint – the experience gave an understanding of how the original carvers used lines, angles, circles, templates and free hand. They comprise 387 of the carvings seen on the symbol stones. Some examples are indistinct but 281 have been drawn – at www.pictish-mithraism.com. A selection is arranged in Appendix 2.

Survival rates for these drawn objects varies with the lowest being the Z-Rod & Double Disc design and the highest the Mirror Case followed closely by the Mirror and Triple Disc. Assuming a fairly even distribution of chips and breaks and material durability across the stones, so no one design is worse affected than another, then perhaps the construction of the design is a key factor in its longevity. It is easier to incise simple circles than the "flame" components on Z-Rods which also tend to be more elaborate with intricate infill. Overall, for 6 of these 12 drawn objects more than 80% of what has been carved has survived.

With the need when interpreting the Mysteries of Mithras to think of several levels – practical, instructional, devotional, spiritual – the same thought process has been given to decoding the Pictish Symbols when placed in the context of Mithraism. The potential for multiple meanings has also been considered.

Where stones are mentioned with a number in brackets e.g. Kirriemuir (2) this is the reference used in the RCAHMS publication – The Pictish Symbol Stones of Scotland.

V-Rod & Crescent

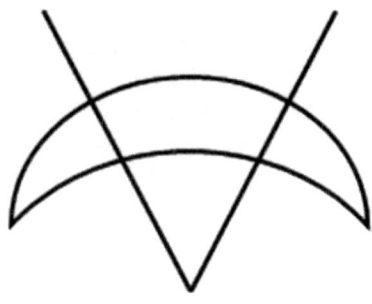

This is the popular, descriptive name for what historically has been determined as two symbols that look like a bent rod and a crescent (particularly influenced, seemingly, by the shape of the crescent moon). This is the most prolifically used symbol on Class 1 and Class 2 stones and is not restricted to any specific geographic area. The shape is undoubtedly like a crescent moon but is never seen in a correct "sky" orientation. Some commentators have thought the V-Rod element looks like bulls' horns.

These are examples of stones with both V- Rod & Crescent and Z-Rod with Double Disc symbols (both licensed images courtesy of National Museums of Scotland, Edinburgh).

Left hand is the Fiscavaig Stone and right hand the Invereen Stone.

The decoration within the crescents and the "flame style", arrow or finial on the rods varies so much that each design is unique. So, starting from a very general pattern (above) there then is no consistency in any detail where a number of stones are to the same design or, indeed, are any sufficiently similar to produce any groups of designs. This tends to suggest the carver only needed to comply with the basic pattern and had a rather broad artistic licence. Conversely, maybe the commissioner of the slab or individual object on it expressed a wish for a particular style of adornment. Either way, this has resulted in our seeing 90 objects following the general pattern, of which 27 are indistinct. 63 separate designs have emerged.

The V-Rod shape is never seen on its own; there is only one instance of it being combined with a symbol other than a Crescent (a Horseshoe/Arch at Migvie).

20 instances of the V-Rod & Crescent are at the top of Class 1 stones. At Advie, Ballintomb, Bourtie, Cairnton, Clach Ard, Daviot, Fyvie, Inveravon (x2), Invereen, Inverurie, Kinblethmont, Kintore Churchyard, Logie Elphinstone (x2), Pabbay, Poolewe, Strathmartine Castle and Tillytarmont (x2).

Latheron

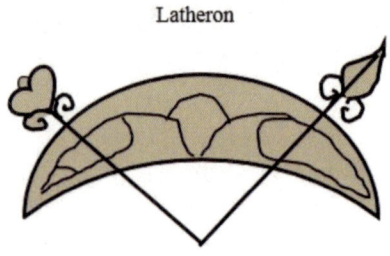

When the crescent shape is with the V-Rod & Crescent it is always orientated as in the Latheron example alongside – except for Deer (the other way round) for which there is an 1800s sketch recording of the stone which has been lost for over 100 years. Maybe the sketching is incorrect. Even the smaller crescent adornments within the main crescent follow the same orientation apart from Bourtie, where the inner crescents are positioned in parallel with the rods and Kintradwell, where the infill is like two back-to-back commas.

Maybe the V-Rod is not a rod at all! As with the Z-Rod there have been suggestions that it is a broken spear signifying death and/or burial. The "rod" has also been referred to as a sceptre (carried by people in authority – monarchs, for example) so this might lead to the V-Rod and Crescent being somehow linked to a king (but why a broken sceptre?). If the V-Rod is not a single rod at all but two items, then an alternative view emerges. Perhaps these are two lines representing something coming to a focal point. Many of the lines on the stones have finials; taken with the line these add direction (in other words directional arrows).

In decoding symbols used in Mithraism there reasonably would be identification of a bull – the crescent shape looks like bull horns. The bull was slain by Mithras – maybe the V-Rod shape is a sword or Persian harpe. The two (bull horns and sword) would amply fit as a Tauroctony Symbol.

However, in the overall analysis there are few carvings of bulls. In fact, 8, of which 6 are associated with Burghead the other two being at Woodwrae with other animals and beasts on a cross slab and Kingsmills, Inverness as a single object on what looks like a Class 1 fragment. Having decided the bull analogy for the crescent was most likely over-emphasised and that Pictish-Mithraism did not perhaps fully use the mystery of the Roman Mithraism Tauroctony, then some other alternatives surfaced.

The general crescent style is the same as a crescent moon except for orientation; turn it clockwise and we see the waxing crescent of the first quarter phase; turning it counter-clockwise and we see the waning crescent of the last quarter. Maybe the carvings are moon phases – but there is not a range of orientations.

As part of the Mysteries of Mithras the moon figures prominently, not least as an initiation grade (Perses) which has the moon as its planet with the harpe (sickle and scythe) and a crescent moon with star as associated symbols.

A suggestion is that the crescent shape looks like a view of the sky and beyond. The infill on some crescents looks like stylised clouds such as the stone at Kinblethmont, near Arbroath.

This would be the "skyward" view across the sea:

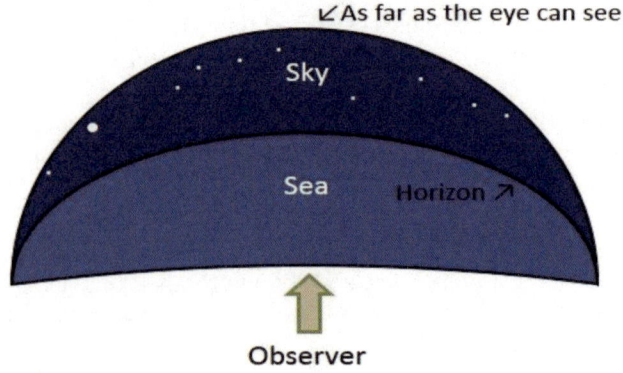

The view across land would be less well defined at the horizon.

Whilst multiple explanations, including depictions of the moon and the Roman Mithraic Tauroctony might be given for the V-Rod and Crescent, in the context of the migration from Roman Mithraism to Pictish-Mithraism there is a composite explanation for this, the most numerous, symbol.

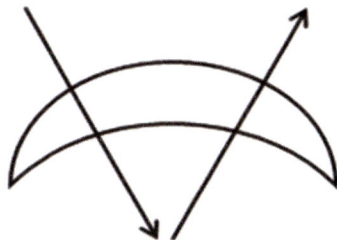

The V-Rod is not a rod but two arrows (left down, right up).

Broomend

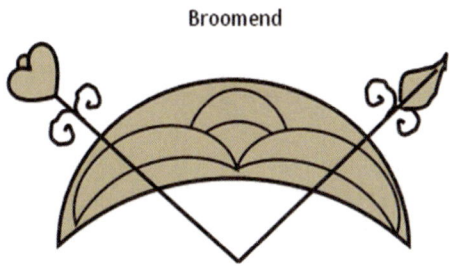

These arrows are stylistically given direction, sometimes with "flames" as used for Z-Rods or with equivalent devices.

If the outer curve of the crescent equates to the furthest skyward view – the firmament / vault of Heaven / sphere of the fixed stars / celestial sphere – then the inner curve is the horizon.

In Mithraism, taking a skyward view, the directional arrows would have suggested the soul travelling from the direction of the fixed celestial sphere via the moving planets at birth and returning via those planets and the celestial sphere on death; in effect into mortality and later into immortality. The symbolism is structured in such a way that the observer can consider himself to be at the focal point looking out to the skyward view (planets and celestial sphere) and imagining the soul's travel.

Taking the analysis a stage further, perhaps the outer curve of the Crescent can be made more specific than "celestial sphere" and be considered to represent the Milky Way – astrologically the home of the soul. Astrologically souls descend on birth through the Gate of Cancer and ascend after death through the Gate of Capricorn – these gates (described by Porphyry as two holes in the sphere of fixed stars) being where the Milky Way and zodiac intersect. The decode for the V-Rod in Pictish-Mithraism as directional arrows aligns with this astrological concept.

"Gates" as holes in the sphere of fixed stars opens up another possibility. Heaven is considered not to be tangible; it is beyond what we can see; it is indefinable. We can see the planets and the celestial sphere (the home of constellations, therefore, including the zodiac). In theology in general, maybe Heaven as the home, or realm, of God or the gods (depending on religious belief) is beyond the celestial sphere. Maybe Heaven is reached via gates, or holes in the "sphere of fixed stars" into a place that is invisible so is undefined.

In terms of Pictish-Mithraism and its symbols, the arrows which represent the travel of the soul are carved such that they neither start nor finish at the edge of the skyward view. If deliberately drawn over the skyward view (without pictorial licence or error) the carver was showing that the soul resides beyond the celestial sphere, in invisible Heaven; it travels across (or through) that sphere to the observer on Earth.

In summary, consistent with the principles of Mithraism, the V-Rods are directional arrows, the angle between them represents the passage of time between the arrival of the soul on birth, into mortality, and its departure on death, into immortality. The Crescent is the skyward view from Earth to the planets and the fixed stars of the celestial sphere – beyond is Heaven. This invisible Heaven – the home of the soul – is beyond the celestial sphere; it is where the directional arrows start and finish.

There is infill on many of the stones – maybe more artistic licence than further symbolism although a recurring theme is sets of arcs like the crescent itself. These arcs and other shapes could represent clouds.

The 14 additional objects in the V-Rod / Crescent object category have not been separately drawn as 13 have similarities with the general crescent plus one example of a V-Rod with a Horseshoe / Arch:

There are 7 Crescent alone objects. Daviot is similar to Tobar na Maor and Clynekirkton (1) V-rod & Crescent designs. Kingoldrum has internal scroll patterns as have St Vigeans (1) and Meigle (6) – all similar to Meigle (4) V-rod & Crescent design. Rosskeen, Little Ferry Links (2) and Breck of Hillwell are indistinct.

In each case of the 4 Double Crescent objects (Kintore, Castle Hill (2), Newton of Lewesk, Ulbster and Dunrobin, Dairy Park) the double crescent is achieved by mirror-imaging between the upper and lower crescents.

The V-rod & Horseshoe / Arch at Migvie mixes two symbols which are decoded and discussed in this chapter. The style of carving used on this symbol stone is different from all others.

The Notched Crescent at Easterton of Roseisle is a plain, filled crescent with a notch in the lower central portion which alternatively could be a horseshoe design.

Mirror

This is one of the best objects for stylistically analysing and grouping but is one of the more difficult to interpret. Of the 62 "mirror" objects visible on symbol stones 8 are indistinct with those that have been drawn having two broad patterns – "ring" (in fact an open circle on a type of base) and "solid". In both patterns the significant objects are a large circle typically with two interconnected circles at the base. In total 21 designs emerged which have been arranged into 5 groups – all shown on the website.

The illustration on the left is of the "ring" pattern from Group 1 and can be seen on 7 stones.

The illustration on the right is of the "solid" pattern from Group 2 and can be seen on 6 stones.

In an ancient Persian context, the "ring" shape itself is like the ring held by Ahura-Mazda and is held by the king, whereby the king is invested with the royal power by the god and is Ahura-Mazda's proxy on Earth (there is an example of this on a wall panel in the British Museum of Darius's investiture). Perhaps the Group 1 designs could be the Double Disc as the concentric arrangements of Earth / planets / celestial sphere linked to the Ring as a form of contract between the people on Earth and God. Group 2 has the Double Disc but linked to a solid circle – maybe this is a less clear version of Group 1 or it could have another meaning. Group 3, however, is more like a depiction of the birth of Mithra from the rock and maybe Group 4 is a simpler version of Group 3. To add to the wide selection, Group 5 has variants of the other groups – each can have an individual explanation such as Picardy has; a suggestion of the Double Disc but to a clearly boundaried solid circle with a central concentric.

Often in standing stone books the Mirror and Mirror Case are described as complementary – hence their names. However, for a Pictish-Mithraism interpretation this is inapplicable – they are neither mirror, nor mirror case but it is convenient, for consistency, to use these terms. The "mirror" in Pictish-Mithraism decoding could comprise one or both sides of the double disc part of the Z-Rod & Double Disc design with the larger circle being the zodiac. A Knockando / Pulvrenan Stone has a similar layout except the centre is dominated by a rather weathered flower type symbol. The Tillytarmont example also has the three concentric circles in the "double disc" part – these are considered to represent the Earth, planets and celestial sphere.

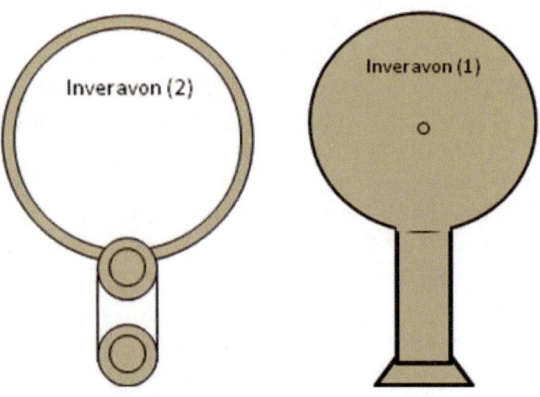

At Inveravon there is one of each Mirror pattern (a "ring" and a "solid"), the solid example being on the stone with the eagle and the Comb with the double row of teeth. For Inveravon Stone 2 the symbol could be a Double Disc (representing the Earth, planets and celestial sphere) either extending out to a larger portrayal of the celestial sphere or to the zodiac. If the latter, then there is a symbolic link between Mithras and the zodiac which the author considers is the general decode for the Mirror Case object. Inveravon Stone 1 is a one-off for a Mirror design and is more like a Mirror Case. However, for this stone it does reflect the style of the Mirror Case, suggesting some artistic licence.

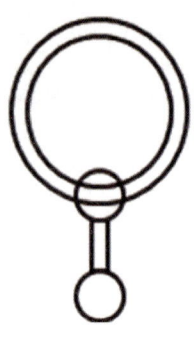

On the assumption that these shapes are mirror-like the conclusion by many authors has tended to be that they have a female association – not least with the supposition of matrilineal succession for Pictish kings. This view has been reinforced by these symbols often being accompanied by a "Comb". Combs are never seen without associated Mirrors – this association of Mirrors and Combs could simplify their interpretation but maybe incorrectly (see the section on Combs).

Although it might be difficult to understand that in Mithraism there is a grade that has female attributes in an all-male cult, it would be easy to sustain the "traditional" Mirror / Comb association and propose that the mirror, mirror case and comb represent the Nymphus Grade which is the second grade in the 7step ladder whereby the initiate becomes the bride of Mithras. With the planet associated with the Nymphus grade being Venus, which is the second planet from the Sun, perhaps there is some significance in the circles. The planet Venus is known as the morning star and relates in Mithraism to Cautes. This prompts further thought on the interpretation of the circles of the Mirror as astronomical bodies and their revolution – particularly applicable to Groups 1 and 2. Astrologically the mirror is a portal to the soul or, more generally, into another dimension – again very applicable to Mithraism.

According to Allen and Anderson the Mirror is almost always placed in the "last or lowermost" position when in combination with other symbols on Class 1 stones. This could be seen as a "southernmost" connection; arguably a Capricorn link could be implied (see more about Capricorn under Pictish Beast).

Whilst not dismissing the prospect of a link with the Nymphus grade, especially after stating that the symbols might have multiple meanings, in the Pictish-Mithraism bigger picture, the Mirror circles can be considered to depict relationships between the zodiac, planets and the Earth.

In each case the large circle is the zodiac – more obvious in the "ring" pattern as that is how the zodiac is shown in Mithras group statuary.

The smaller circles, especially where there are concentric ones, are very similar to the circles on the Z-Rod & Double Disc objects. Where there are circles connected by "waist" effect lines such as in Group 1, item 3 (Clatt, Daviot, Keith Hall etc.) and Group 2, item 3 (Rhynie Old Church 1, Dunrobin Dairy Park etc.) the impression is of a solid ring that has been cut through (as with the Double Disc in the Z-Rod & Double Disc Symbol). This similarity is even greater in Group 1, Item 1(Tillytarmont).

Where the Double Disc meets or overlaps the zodiac circle this point can be considered to be Capricorn – consistent with Capricorn in the south (versus Cancer in the north as the point where the soul comes from the Celestial Sphere). Additionally, this shape combination could represent a form of contract between Mithras and the universe and all it contains.

Whether "ring" or "solid" it is still the "zodiac circle" being depicted and not just the sun and moon as suggested by some.

Group 3 has design features similar to the Mirror Case. They are in the Mirror section here and in Appendix A on the website because that is how they are labelled in popular texts. Perhaps there is a dual meaning for the Meigle, Maiden Stone and Collace examples. This "duality" is explored in the Mirror Case section.

Z-Rod & Double Disc

Z-Rod & Double Disc is the popular name for what historically has been determined as two (or more) shapes that look like a Z shaped rod and, in the main, two separate but inter-connected circles or discs. In fact, the Z-Rods in the Z-Rod & Double Disc configuration comprise a reverse-Z but the "Z" description is traditional and convenient. It is most unlikely that the carver even considered the notion of a Z or reversed Z – it is just the way the symbol was created. The Z-Rod is never seen on its own (just like the V-Rod) – it is combined with either the Double Disc formation or with a Serpent or a Notched Rectangle. This tends to confirm a particular meaning conferred to the "Z", or its components, which is not adversely modified (or lost) when combined with other symbols – more likely enhancing their meaning.

To decode this composite symbol it is useful, initially, to disassemble into components. Just as the V-Rod is not, in the context of Pictish-Mithraism, a rod at all but directional arrows, the "arms" of the Z can be considered to be directional arrows. In many instances there are directional finials; generally, they are more elaborate compared with the V-Rods – in fact, more floriated. Suggestions have been made that these might represent lightning and that does have a Mithraic context with the Leo Grade. Alternatively, these shapes may have multiple meanings.

This is the third most prolifically used symbol on Pictish Stones and, like V-Rods & Crescents, not restricted to any specific geographic area. Several stones have both V-Rod and Z-Rod symbols on them, often juxtaposed as on the Invereen and Fiscavaig Stones, as shown in the previous section on V-Rods and Crescents. This juxta-positioning is discussed in the section on symbol groups.

With the Z-Rod / Double Disc object category being almost as numerous as the V-Rod / Crescent object category immediately there is a supposition that these are symbols of important meaning and both are geographically well distributed. However, unlike the V-Rod & Crescent accounting for 87% within its object category the Z-Rod & Crescent is only 57% within its object category. This suggests a fundamental difference in how the objects are decoded, with the V-Rod & Crescent together portraying a very specific message and the Z-Rod and the Double Disc components sometimes combined with others, maybe giving a wider range of messages.

Most examples of this symbol have the orientation shown here in this general pattern. A few are rotated 90 degrees counter-clockwise and only one (discovered so far) is rotated 45 degrees counter-clockwise.

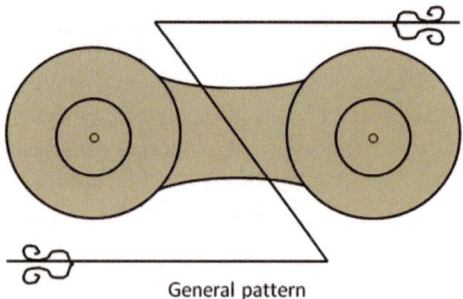

General pattern

What they all have in common is symmetry about the axis at right angles to the circles and lines connecting the circles that are almost always curved into their centre line. This could be specific styling, even decoratively stylistic, but is consistent. Unless there was a recorded "standard" for the symbols or pure coincidence the alternative is that each engraver understood a specific construction to show whatever the circles or discs were intended to depict. The carving on the stones is pictorially two dimensional (even where some Class 2 carvings are "raised" in relief) not using projections, such as orthogonal, or other techniques to imply depth or distance or to give perspective.

However, with the centre line symmetry and the "waist" effect of the curved lines joining the outer circles there appears to be a 3-D representation of a solid torus cross-section (a cut through ring doughnut or bagel shape). This applies to those double discs with the same content in each disc (which is the majority) including those that have off-centre circles (such as Invereen, Struan and Congash).

This is how the 3-D effect is created on a 2-dimensional surface:

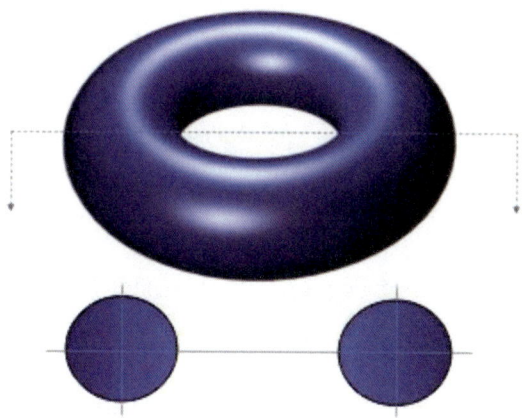

A ring doughnut shape is created by taking a circle then sweeping it vertically through 360°.

This is a cross-section through this shape.

It is 2-dimensional, looks like 2 circles and there is no suggestion of depth.

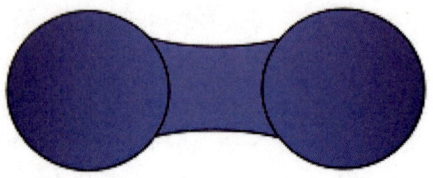

The 2-D view can be given a three-dimensional aspect to appear more like a cut through dough-ring by connecting the circles with the curved lines. This "waist" gives the 3-D effect. Looking at the construction (on the previous page) in reverse, the 2-D drawing with a 3-D effect can be translated back into the dough-ring shape. This "waisted" shape has important implications in the decoding of the Double Disc symbols.

In researching the 56 objects that broadly follow the general pattern above, 29 were found to be too indistinct to be drawn. Examples not drawn include: Kirriemuir (2) – double disc with a rod terminating in a three leaf clover style motif; St Vigeans (1) and Meigle – "Z-rod" reversed resembling a conventional Z; Edderton – no central circle in one end and non-concentric in the opposite end plus right-angled "Z"; Clach Ard – non-concentric circles at both ends; Fiscavaig – no inner concentric circles, one rod terminates in a three leaf clover style motif; Rodney's Stone – circles at each end surround "Celtic" style patterns. Wantonwells is indistinct but appears to have discs with 7 radial segments. Dingwall has offset concentric circles like Invereen & Struan but with indistinct rods. However, 26 have been drawn and 18 designs emerged which are distinguished by the variants of "flame" numbers and directions.

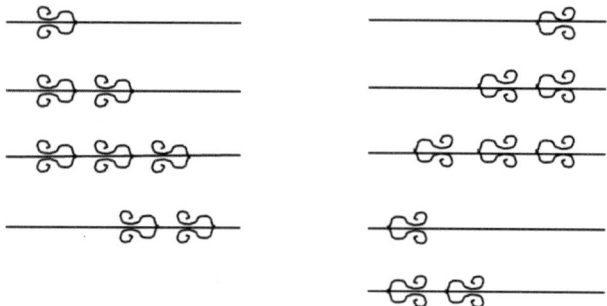

All of the Z-Rods terminate in "flame" patterns which appear to be more than just decorative finials. The adjacent illustration shows the variants for the left and right side horizontal parts of the "Z". There is symmetry top to bottom in a third of cases, maybe not a high figure but enough to suggest there may be a reason for such symmetry. There is a high consistency in the shape of the flame elements with only Tullich being noticeably different but that may be more due to the carver than a particular reason for a slightly different shape – the rest of that slab has some inaccurate carving, especially the Mirror circles.

With the stones being the terrestrial part of the Open Air Mithraeum described in Chapter 7 (Stones and Distant Views) then the Z-Rod combinations are very significant. Mithras in known paintings and sculptures (most especially the Tauroctony) is a central figure accompanied by Cautes and Cautopates. In Mithraism, Cautes represents the morning star and Cautopates the evening star. The morning star is associated with the east (bringing dawn and light at the beginning of the day). The evening star is associated with the west (bringing dusk and night at the end of the day). In pictures and sculptures Cautes and Cautopates are holding torches (they are often called the torch bearers). Cautes typically to the right of Mithras holds a lit torch upwards, Cautopates to Mithras's left holds an extinguishing torch downwards – again reinforcing the symbolism as morning and evening. Close study of the symbols on the Pictish Symbol Stones shows many examples where the seemingly floriated ends of the upper part of the Z-Rod appear to be flames from torches; hence the "flame" comments above. Other than direction, the variants of "flame" styles seem artistic with no further meaning.

The torches mark the beginning and the end of the day so the innermost parts of the torches are connected by the joining line of the "Z". Typically, this connection lies across the centre line of the circles or discs. Several suggestions have been made about the circles – sun and moon, other paired items in harmony or tension (like yin/yang), Heaven and hell, decorative. An alternative could be the sun (sol) with Mithras (Sol Invictus) – in Mithraism there is a distinct difference. The Sun is one of the planets being, in some interpretations, located halfway between the Earth and the celestial sphere giving equitable illumination (and heat) to the planets on either side of its circular path. Sol Invictus (more specifically recorded as Deus Sol Invictus – the unconquerable Sun God), is the creator of the universe, the Mithras who knows about the precession of the equinoxes, the god who has the power to rotate the entire universe. He is in balance with the sun hence the two are shown together.

In the pre-Roman versions of Mithras, Mithra is the god of contracts; in the Roman version he, Mithras, can be considered to be in contract with the god Sol, the Sun. Alternatively, or in parallel, the discs could be the universe (especially in concentric-circle or so-called "circle and dot" versions) with the Earth at the centre.

With representations of the torches of Mithras' companions, Cautes and Cautopates, prospectively found as the floriated rods in the Z-Rod and Double Disc Symbol then it seems reasonable that Mithras should also be represented. With his power (in Mithraism) to rotate the universe and his status as a god then he would be central to the Z-Rod symbolism but arguably outside it.

Theologically a god would be beyond the universe suggesting that Mithras would be connected to Cautes and Cautopates but beyond the celestial sphere.

Cautes (picture courtesy of Wikipedia commons)

Cautopates (picture courtesy of Wikipedia commons)

Cautes and Cautopates have further symbolism. In addition to their representing the beginning and end of the day (during which the sun shines) they also signify the spring and autumn equinoxes. In the Tauroctony pictures and sculptures they are usually shown with their legs crossed – Cautes left over right with the left pointing away from Mithras; Cautopates right over left with the right pointing away from Mithras. The crossed legs could symbolise the crossing of the celestial and ecliptic equators at the time of the equinoxes; the different crossing formats distinguishing the two equinoxes. This is arguably an additional symbolism for the arrow parts of the "Z" giving this symbol grouping a daily meaning (morning and evening) plus a 6-monthly meaning at the equinoxes. Additionally, making a zodiac relationship, Cautes is in Taurus and Cautopates is in Scorpio.

If a Mithraeum had the monuments in the east end (the cult niche) then an observer's view to the east from the narthex would typically (but not always in all known Mithraea) have Cautes on our right (Mithras left) and Cautopates on our left (Mithras right). The sun rises (marking the day's start) in the east, traverses south then sets in the west – at equinox time these events are 180° apart. Looking straight on at a Z-Rod & Double Disc on a symbol stone, the upper floriated or flame part of the Z-Rod could represent Cautes and the lower part Cautopates. With many outdoor stones prospectively having been moved from their original locations e.g. within churchyards, it is difficult to assess whether there was a specific directional orientation when the stones were first erected. However, this is being further investigated by the author.

Placing the components of this symbol into a Pictish-Mithraism context, the Z-Rod is not a rod but two interconnected arrows, generally with flame patterns, representing the torches of Cautes and Cautopates (Mithras's companions seen in the statuary of the Tauroctony) with the "reversed Z" enabling their interconnection.

Cautes is the symbol of life, light and day; Cautopates is the symbol of death, darkness and night (not as unmitigated evils but as a necessary prelude to immortality). One faces east towards the morning star the other west towards the evening star – one's torch is alight the other extinguishing signifying the beginning and end of the day; they further depict the spring and autumn equinoxes.

The connecting part of the "Z" is firstly the day, secondly the months between the equinoxes, thirdly time itself – the start is connected to the finish.

As a two-dimensional representation, the circles or discs can be multi-depiction – the sun (sol) and moon (luna) in harmony or tension; the sun (sol) and Mithras (Deus Sol Invictus – the unconquerable Sun God, the creator of the universe) in balance.

However, the symbol takes on much greater meaning when the Double Disc is seen not just as two discs but, with the "waist" effect lines in between, as a three-dimensional representation of the cross-section of a solid dough-ring type shape. There is symmetry between the sets of concentric circles that form the Double Disc (consistent with the cross-section of a dough-ring shape) – the Earth is in the middle of the disc then the moving planets then the fixed celestial sphere. Collectively these are the elements of a contained universe. Heaven is beyond that material universe with Mithras externally able to rotate the universe from outside – hence the Z-Rod overlays what we call the Double Disc that is a representation of the contained universe. Arrows representing Mithras's supporters, Cautes and Cautopates, are also shown external to the contained universe.

Additionally, the principle of the travel of the soul from Heaven via the celestial sphere and planets (as embodied in the V-Rod & Crescent symbol) could be explained using the directional arrows of the Z-Rod.

Furthermore, the entire "Z" shape could be seen as a serpent which, as a set of constellations (principally Hydra) forms a connection between Cancer and Capricorn (the gateways of the soul).

The "Z" is overlaid across the cross-sectional representation of the universe (Double Disc) that contains the Earth, the planets and the constellations (on the celestial sphere):

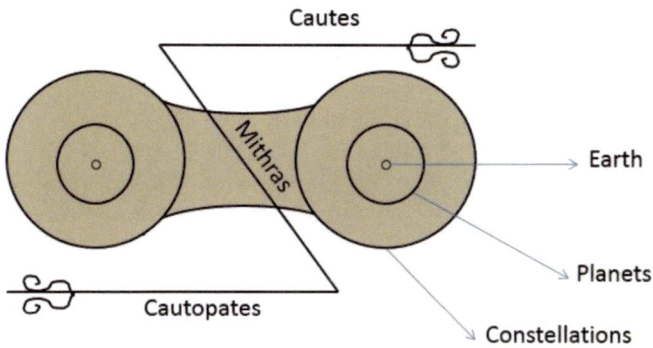

This symbol acts as the platform for deeper explanation and understanding via the Mithraic Grades; for example, some circles are infilled with 7circles, the number of planets (at the time).

The symbolism on the Pictish Stone is structured in such a way that the observer can use this solid, terrestrial part of the Open Air Mithraeum to guide towards the truly open part that is the sky and beyond. The observer's presence may be small but he is part of it; all the changes are happening around him – again, as with the V-Rod, he can become the focal point.

Looking at the circles or discs in more detail there are many hidden symbolic details, many of which link to Mithraism. The discs on the Dyce Stones are three concentric circles – arguably the Earth at the centre (the "dot"), the first circle being the planets and the second the celestial sphere. On stones at Inverurie Kirkyard and East Balhaggardy there is a dot and three concentric circles – perhaps the above three constituents are there (and no more) with the dot showing from the centre point of a compass with the next circle out being the Earth; the Keith Hall Stone is another example of this configuration. In other words, the Earth is being given a greater presence than just a dot.

Occasionally the circles or discs are in-filled. On the Wantonwells, Insch Stone each circle has curved lines like a counter-clockwise rotating turbine. There is a dot with a closed in inner circle and an outer circle. The 7curved lines are between the two circles. 7is significant – the number of planets and of Mithraic Grades.

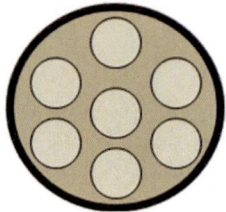

An Aberlemno Stone also has a "7" connection – each of the circles contains 7small circles (detail alongside); the Glenferness Stone is likewise. Whilst the Nigg Stone also has small circles within a larger one it is highly stylised with an additional circle within the envelope of the larger circle and the space where the inner line of the "Z" crosses.

The Dunnichen Stone has another variant on the theme – 7 serially connected filigree style curls between the inner and outer circles; maybe the dot is a centre point, the Earth the inner circle, the planets the middle curled circle and the outer the celestial sphere. 7 stars can be construed to be the Plough which is the Bear which moves and turns the heavens around.

Two additional designs are part of the Z-Rod / Double Disc Object Category:

The Notched Double Disc at Newton House has a notch similar to those on the stone at Inchrya. However, unlike all other Double Discs (with and without Z-rods) it is not symmetrical – the single notch is out of the lower part of the left hand disc.

Artistic licence would be required to construct anything meaningful from the indistinct carving at what is classified as the Z-rod & Rectangle at Cullaird, Scaniport.

Pictish Beast

As a stylised animal the so-called Pictish Beast stands alone – by reason of its popularity on the stones and by being different from all the other animals on the stones whether zoomorphic or otherwise. Like many of the foregoing groupings of symbols it has a fairly well "standardised" design on the stones – both Class 1 and Class 2 – so it, like them, endured in use for about 300/500 years. Only one stylised drawing is shown here to the left. There is no need for more as they follow a general pattern except for being left or right facing and of varying angle of incline. They all feature a "lappet" and typically a dolphin- like snout (hence why they are sometimes referred to as "Pictish Dolphin". Of the 51 examples over 2/3rds are right facing with exceptions at Fyvie, Balluderon, Largo, Tealing, Glenferness, Scoonie, Nigg, Shandwick, Golspie, Dunfallandy, Ulbster and Meigle (5). All have plain bodies except the right facing, weathered beast at Glenferness which has some interlace and Brodie with Celtic continuous line styling and the left facing Nigg "beast" which too has Celtic styling but of a more angular line than at Brodie. Navidale is so worn that the carving can barely be seen.

Various descriptions have been given to this symbol ranging from the non-committal Pictish Beast to the very specific Pictish Dolphin and less practical Pictish Elephant. Benchmarking is almost impossible – but not quite. Like the V-Rod and Z-Rod, the design is localised broadly to the North East of Scotland but, unlike the Z-Rod and V-Rod there are known shape similarities elsewhere.

In Assyrian history there is a beast called "mushhushshu" or sirrush who was supposed to have protected many of the supreme gods such as Marduk, the city God of Babylon.

Mushhushshu

Time wise, Marduk came to prominence around 1500 BCE – the same period as Persian Mithra and prior to the monotheism of Zoroastrianism. Mushhushshu had associations with other Gods; it is described as "crypto-zoological" made from a combination of animals that could never have existed in nature. Maybe too much of a coincidence or completely unconnected; maybe a design cue? If not a coincidence, then this could suggest a linkage between the knowledge of the stone builders and a people who lived about 2,000 years before – in which case there is some difficulty in determining how that knowledge travelled – or that there was some form of continuum to enable that over two millennia.

Turning to Mithraic related possibilities there are many options. It is tempting to think of the Pictish Beast shape prospectively fitting a choice from the Leontocephalous (lion headed beast), the serpent (whether the constellation Serpens or Hydra or, terrestrially, a snake) or the lion (as in the Leo Grade or as symbolising a powerful beast). In Persian and Roman Mithraism, the soul travels via the 7 planets in its journey to the celestial sphere then to Heaven with the Leontocephalous alongside the eighth gate (the gate to Heaven).

In decoding the more numerous Pictish Symbols it is important to think about the definition of "gate" – "an opening permitting passage through an enclosure, means of access, entrance, leads to a place…". So a gate can enable movement between one place and another. Therefore, when a gate is encountered something ahead of it is expected. In Mithraic terms, on death the soul leaves the person and travels towards the first gate (a planet) with the functionality of the gate giving the expectation of reaching it, passing through then going to a next stage (another planet). This sequence is repeated until the soul has traversed every planet and after leaving the last one it goes towards the sphere of fixed stars (the celestial sphere) where it has the expectation of encountering an eighth gate – the final one which gives access to Heaven and the end of its journey.

This final gate is described by Porphyry as one of the holes in the sphere of fixed stars, astrologically the Gate of Capricorn. The gate through which the soul moves from Heaven towards its planetary journey on birth is Cancer – following the reverse steps to the one described above on death.

Tracing this journey on death has been used to arrive at Capricorn and to consider how it is depicted – perhaps it is the inspiration for the Pictish Beast.

The story of Capricornus originated with the Babylonians and Sumerians. The Sumerians knew it as the goat-fish, or SUHUR-MASH-HA, while the Babylonian star catalogues dating back to 1000 BC mention the Constellation as MUL.SUHUR.MAŠ, also meaning "goat fish." In the early Bronze Age, Capricornus marked the winter solstice and, in modern astrology, Capricorn's rule still begins on the first day of winter. Generally depicted as terrestrial animal in the front part and in the hind part as aquatic animal, the Makara is a sea creature in Hindu mythology and is the astrological sign of Capricorn which is also known as the "sea goat".

Drawings of Capricorn and the Pictish Beast are remarkably similar -

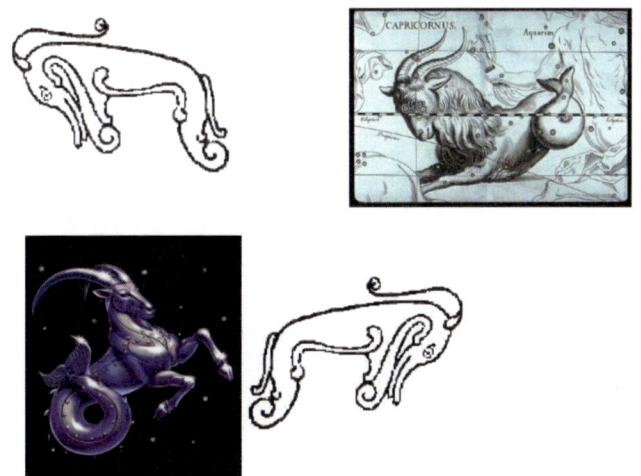

Enhancing the decode for this symbol is the Pictish Beast's position relative to other symbols in those cases where there are groupings. On Class 1 stones the beast is often next to the V-Rod, usually beneath it, and next to the arch, usually below it. On Class 2 stones the beast is more randomly placed, when on the cross side it is typically high up. These relational positions are explored in Appendix B on the website concluding with the realisation that the connection is the Capricorn constellation – the Pictish Beast representing the sea goat that is Capricorn, the directional arrows of the V-Rod & Crescent being the travel of the soul on birth and death, the Crescent representing the Milky Way – the home of the soul and the Capricorn constellation being intersected by the Milky Way creating one of the Gates of the Gods through which the soul travels. In addition, and further enhancing what is a fundamental discovery linking several symbols together was establishing the relationship between the zodiac, planets and Earth in the decode of the Mirror, above.

In Mithraic terms, therefore, Capricorn can be seen as the linkage between the V-Rod & Crescent, the Mirror and the Pictish Beast symbols.

The arrows comprising the V-Rod represent the travel of the soul from and to Heaven via the planets and the celestial sphere. The Crescent as well as showing the skyward view across the horizon portrays the Milky Way. Capricorn and Cancer mark the extremities of the Milky Way and lie near it. Capricorn astrologically is the Gate of the Gods through which the soul travels on its return following death and into immortality.

In the Mirror symbols where the Double Disc meets or overlaps the zodiac circle this point can be considered to be Capricorn – consistent with Capricorn in the south.

From its shape and positioning, the Pictish Beast can be seen as the sea goat which is the sign of Capricorn. On a symbol stone it could act as a "pointer" to that constellation in the skyward view and enable, with reference to the V-Rod & Crescent, an explanation of the travel of the soul back to Heaven on death. With a fundamental Mithraic belief of the soul enduring in immortality on a person's death the significance of signposting the portal to Heaven is reinforced.

These involved decodes show the degree and depth to which symbols have been encoded. In other words, when the symbol is far removed from what it seems then a deeper drill down is needed because the representation is in layers. Whoever decided on the Pictish Beast to depict a constellation must have had a very advanced knowledge of Mithraism and a highly-developed capability to layer its concealment. This concealment of the mystery aspect of the cult is well exemplified here and the need for verbally teaching initiates is realised.

Comb

Of the 40 Comb objects identified 6 are indistinct. So 34 have been drawn resulting in 22 distinct designs emerging, which have been arranged into 4 groups. Several Combs do not have recognisable "teeth" as such so look more like Decorated Rectangles. In keeping with not re-classifying objects from how they are generally recorded in readily available texts, there has been no re-allocation between the Comb and Decorated Rectangle in the lists of Objects By Location in Appendix F at www.pictish-mithraism.com. That said, it is worth covering these differences and similarities now by considering how the four groups of Combs have been created. Group D is very straightforward – all examples are double-sided "combs" i.e. teeth on opposing surfaces, and Group C single-sided i.e. teeth on only one surface. Group B has as a common feature curved shapes on the top of the design with 3 of the 7 having several parallel lines beneath which look like "teeth"; the remaining four have rectangle shapes in the lower portion so look somewhat like Decorated Rectangles.

Finally, in Group A all the shapes are rectangle based, four with what one might call "contained teeth" in other words kept within rectangular outers then two designs which are on Keith Hall, Drimmies, Drumbuie and Sandside Stones which are just rectangular boxes with no "teeth". These latter do not really fall into the Decorated Rectangle category at all so are the odd ones out but nonetheless are recorded in texts as Combs.

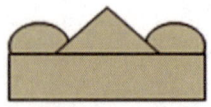
Nether Corskie

Having noted the traditional Mirror / Comb combination and concluded a symbolic Mithraic context for the Mirror, it is now necessary to see what the research into Mithraism might suggest for the Comb. The complication arises with so many objects being referred to as "comb" but without the attributes of such an item. 6 of the 22 designs are not comb-like but maybe have other meanings – so far not apparent. For example, Nether Corskie (alongside) is in this category.

Combs with "teeth" on one side are Clach Ard with 5, Tillytarmont with 7, Inveravon Stone 2 with 8 and Collace with 7. Those with "teeth" on both sides are Cullaird with 5, Inveravon Stone 1 with 7, Meigle Stone 1 with 13, Birse with 7 and a symbol design that has "ends" beyond the "teeth" with a varying number of "teeth". This last item ranges from The Maiden Stone example with 21 teeth to Kinnedar with 9 and Wester Denoon with 7 and some others.

The significance of the number 7 in Roman Mithraism – planets, grades etc. – and the representation of planets in other symbols, for example, on the Double Discs with Z-Rods, leads to wondering whether the Combs have a hidden "7" meaning. If there is then the Combs that do not have an exact "7" need also to be explained.

Perhaps sculptors in some instances were not always given an exact specification to use a specific number so may have improvised. Alternatively, a requirement could have been to use a comb type design but to obscure the number of "teeth".

For those that do have 7 teeth – Tillytarmont, Collace, Inveravon Stone 1, Wester Denoon and Birse or multiple of 7 such as The Maiden Stone with 21 and Monifieth with 14 then an explanation can be given.

Inveravon Stone 1 Comb

On Pictish Stones the Comb can allude to the Mithraic belief that the soul takes several steps, in fact 7, via the planets between the celestial sphere and the Earth at one's birth (into mortality) and the 7 steps back the way to immortality on one's death. There are 7 Mithraic grades and there are 7 planets (at the time including the sun and moon). The "teeth" could be a used as a counter to assist the explanation in talking an initiate through the levels – those symbols with teeth on one side for the two-way journey, with teeth on both sides on a central bar explaining, separately, the two journeys.

Combs are seen with associated Mirrors perhaps reinforcing a meaning, such as the concept of the steps via the planets from the Comb and the planets as part of the lower concentric rings from the Mirror. When a V-Rod is adjacent the principle of soul travel then has an inter-symbol reinforcement across three symbols – V-Rod, Comb and Mirror.

Whilst authors have given the names Comb and Mirror to these symbols, maybe the original carvers used these shapes to obscure their meaning.

Serpent / Snake

In the object category of "Serpent" (also called Snake) 5 of the 21 objects identified are indistinct leaving 21 which have yielded 17 designs. Not all are Serpents alone.

This category includes 6 designs that have a form of Z-Rod across a serpent (almost half the known serpent/snake objects) where the line connecting the arrows is horizontal or almost horizontal (shown in Appendix A on the website as Group 2). In Group 3 there are 3 examples of a single arrow across a serpent and one (classified in "Others") where the Serpent is shown vertically with the Z-Rod in line.

Here are some examples of the different formats for Serpents on Pictish Stones:

Aberlemno Roadside 1 Serpent/Snake

Newton House Serpent/Snake

Logieriat (1) Serpent/Snake

There is no particular consistency in the orientation of the Serpents on the stones regarding which way the head and tail are facing but they all have two or more body curves and distinct head and tail ends – there is no doubt what the carving is.

In Roman Mithraism the Serpent is present in the Tauroctony sculptures such as the one in the British Museum where the snake is on the flank of the bull, drinking its blood just beneath Mithras' dagger. On a relief in Modena, Northern Italy Mithras is shown as the time-god with a Serpent intertwining his body with its head above his. Mithras has been referred to as the God of Infinite Time with a key predecessor being a lion-headed, human bodied, winged time – god called Aion by the Greeks and Zervan in Persian literature but known in Mithraic terms as Leontocephalous Kronos (the personification of endless time). The latter links back to Zoroastrian teachings with which there are Mithraic (Persian version) linkages. Also, these lion-headed statues are entwined by a Serpent with, typically, 7 coils (maybe an allusion to the 7 planets and 7 associated Mithraic grades).

Because the Serpent casts its skin annually it was considered to be a symbol of regeneration. In Roman tradition snakes were seen as tokens of life beyond the grave. Snakes are also said to represent wisdom.

Turning briefly to some astronomical connections, the serpent in the context of the constellations can be Hydra, Serpens or Draco.

Hydra as one of the 88 modern constellations stretches from Libra to Canis Minor (over 90° of the Celestial Sphere) but in the period when the equinoxes were in Taurus and

Scorpio (circa 4000 BCE to 2000 BCE) Hydra was considered to extend further by including Sextans, Crater and Corvus; more like 180°. The origins of the Mithraic Mysteries relate back to this time period so this notion of an extended hydra is relevant. Also, the serpent has been associated with the brightness in the Milky Way – a connection perhaps with the soul's exit and entry points of Cancer and Capricorn.

Considering the profile of the serpent (snake, hydra etc.) in the symbolism of Roman Mithraic statues and paintings it is maybe surprising to see so few of these shapes on the Pictish Stones. But, maybe not – faced with the ability directly to see this shape in the Open Air Mithraeum perhaps there is less of a need to depict it on the stones. To the knowledgeable the Serpent formation can be seen in the sky at night.

Decoding the Serpent symbol in the context of a transition from Roman to Pictish-Mithraism reveals several possibilities. On Pictish Stones the Serpent on its own (that is, without rods or arrows across it) could represent the rod of Asclepius (single serpent) or the staff of Hermes (two intertwined serpents known as the Caduceus which in Roman mythology was carried by Mercury the messenger of the gods). The Roman Mithraic Corax grade has Mercury as its associated planet – hence another linkage to the snake or serpent. The Leontocephalous (lion headed human) statues have intertwined snakes.

The so-called Pictish Beast is another symbol potentially with a connection with a beast from Persian mythology – the Mushhushshu, also known as the furious snake – which has an association with the Hydra constellation.

Not discounting the foregoing but by focusing on just one of the symbols in the Serpent object category, it is useful to consider the components in Group 2 – a form of Z-Rod across a Serpent with a line connecting arrows at each end. Examples of these are on stones such as the Brandsbutt Stone; the Picardy Stone; St Vigeans; Drumbuie and Newton House examples. In the section above on Z-Rods & Double Discs it was noted that in almost all cases the line shapes are the reverse of a Z (they have been called Z-Rods for convenience). In the case of those Serpents with what is a "Z" shape across them the "Z" lines and snake are on the same axis – a 90° rotation is needed to equate to the "Z". What the components of the Z comprise in Mithraic terms is described above – basically the torch bearers Cautes and Cautopates connected together by a line representing the day, the 6 months between the equinoxes and time itself.

The Serpent has several interpretations in Pictish-Mithraism as derived from Roman Mithraism. When crossed by a Z-rod it reflects the constellations connecting Cautes and Cautopates who represent the equinoxes. In the context of the ladder with 7steps or gates the goal when the soul returns on mortal death to gain immortality is, in fact, the eighth gate which can be represented by the head of the snake beyond the spheres of the 7planets and in the celestial sphere. A snake is wrapped round a lion-headed figure know as a Leontocephalous. The Mithraic Corax grade could also be alluded to by the serpent – that first grade has Mercury as its associated Planet and Mercury is often depicted holding a Caduceus in his role as the messenger of the gods.

Mirror Case

There are 19 Mirror Case objects plus one that is a Notched Mirror Case. One design looks more like a Tuning Fork; the remainder (18) are quite distinct. Two broad patterns emerged – "hollow", that is with an open circle on a base, and "solid". The 17 designs are arranged into 3 groups.

On the assumption that these shapes are mirror-like the conclusion has tended to be that they have a female association. This has been reinforced by these symbols often being linked to the Mirror being accompanied by a Comb. Undoubtedly the shapes accord with Roman style mirrors in use not only in the first millennium CE but centuries before. As with the Mirror there is again the possibility of decoding this symbol as something to do with the Nymphus Grade, the second in the 7step ladder whereby the initiate becomes the bride of Mithras. With the associated planet being Venus perhaps we should be looking for an astronomical interpretation.

Group 1 Mirror Case designs are of the solid pattern variety with concentric circles most notably in the Inverurie (1), Westfield and Knocknagael examples each of which has a small central dot or circle, an intermediate circle plus the outer one. All of these bear a strong resemblance to the Discs with the Z-Rods – a comparison is below:

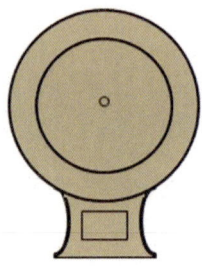

Inverurie (1) Mirror Case

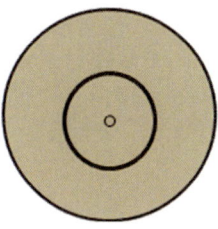

Disc detail from Eassie Z-Rod & Double Disc

Group 2 designs are also of the solid pattern but they have small circles of varying numbers on designs each of which is unique.

Ardnilly has 4 small circles arranged within triangles in a tilted square. Both Inverurie (2) and Drumbuie (2) have 4 small circles within the main circular portion of the symbol and a central small circle; additionally, Inverurie (2) has a small circle on either side of the supporting base. Dyce has two sets of 3 small circles plus another central one – altogether 7 small circles. Inveravon (1) has a more elaborate construction with a central portion not dissimilar to Drumbuie with an added outer area with partially circular lobes (10 in all) each with a small circle. Examples of 4 dots or circles could represent seasons, elements or winds.

Group 3 designs are all hollow, each having a slightly differing style of base supporting the ring. Two that have not been placed in groups are the Newton of Lewesk non-concentric design and the Sandside Notched Mirror Case.

If the rings are deconstructed their decoding may be made easier. Firstly, a common feature for all the Mirror Cases is the supporting base. The hollow and solid patterns for the upper, circular parts give another two distinctive components. By looking to Mithraic iconography and statues there are shapes that align with the Mirror Cases – two, in fact. Mithras was in legend born from a rock, more precisely born from a cosmic egg appearing from a rock.

Additionally, the Mithraic beliefs are portrayed in sculptures and paintings with Mithras stepping out of the rock with the globe in one hand alluding to a cosmic event, touching the zodiac and holding the world in Atlas-like fashion. On a relief at St Aubin in France, the gods of the four winds and four elements are present to honour the birth of Mithras – the ruler of the cosmos.

In the Great North Museum in Newcastle there is a sculpture (from Housesteads on Hadrian's Wall – picture courtesy of GNM) of Mithras being born from the cosmic egg from the rock and holding the zodiac in his hands.

This is of great significance in decoding the Mirror Case and, to an extent, the Mirror designs on the Pictish Stones.

Mithras being born from the Cosmic Egg (stone from Housesteads Mithraeum). Photograph – author, with kind permission of the Society of Antiquaries of Newcastle upon Tyne collection, Great North Museum: Hancock.

This sculpture was once in a Mithraeum on Hadrian's Wall and so has an established relevance to Roman Mithraism which tracks across into Pictish-Mithraism. The rock birth would have been a fundamental point to make to an initiate – the start of Mithras' life on Earth. The grip on the zodiac would have enabled his connection with the cosmos. That grip looks more than static; could it be he is being shown poised to rotate the zodiac and universe.

Looking at some of the Mirror Case objects one can see how the components of the sculpture shown above could be translated into Pictish Symbols. First of all using the Tillytarmont and South Ronaldsay design the combination of Mithras appearing from the rock and holding the zodiac could have been explained from this object. Arguably there is an allusion to arms being outstretched in the dough-ring shape as well as the 360° of the zodiac. From the Group 1 set ("Solid" pattern) the example from Knocknagael suggests the birth from the rock with some added symbolism. That addition is the set of concentric circles which are typically seen with the Z-Rods – the Earth, planet and zodiac/cosmos/celestial sphere/universe could be explained to an initiate of Pictish-Mithraism not only by looking at the stone but the sky beyond. If we add in an example from the Mirror object category, on this occasion from The Maiden Stone, the same combination of rock birth and zodiac plus the elements of the Z-Rod Disc appear. This explanation for the latter design reinforces the difficulty in separately decoding the meaning of some of the Mirror and Mirror Case object – maybe there is a duality of purpose.

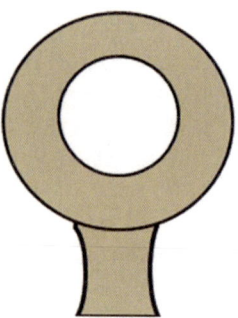

Tillytarmont & South Ronaldsay Mirror Case

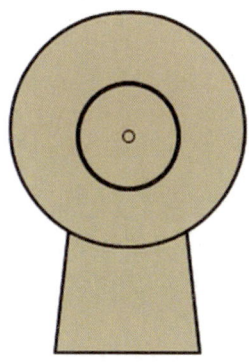

Knocknagael Mirror Case

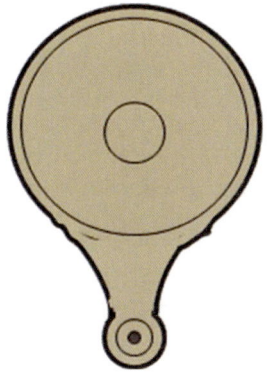

Maiden Stone Mirror Case

The Mirror Case components can be seen in Roman Mithraic sculpture and show a combination of the rock birth of Mithras and his supporting the universe by holding the zodiac – potentially to rotate the universe (contained within the zodiac). The carving of these objects onto the symbol stones shows a straightforward translation into Pictish-Mithraism and complement the decode for the Z-Rod & Double Disc.

Double Disc

These designs are similar to those found with Z-Rods. They are less numerous with 18 objects found that follow a general pattern. 5 are indistinct resulting in 12 separate designs of which 3 are decorated.

Only 3 designs have all the components seen in the Double Discs with Z-Rods – those at Westfield (Falkland), Drumbuie (1) and Inchrya each having the set of three concentric circles representing the Earth, planets and celestial sphere beyond. Woodwrae has the theme of the concentric circles but they are all grouped together in the outer part of the disc and Golspie again has the three circles but evenly spaced. The remainder have only one inner circle and in three designs there is what appears to be purely decorative infill with swirl type patterns (these may have some contextual allusion but this has, so far, eluded the author).

Unlike the Double Discs with Z-Rods, this one has several styling variations compared with the general pattern. The Monifieth design has two concentric circles in the band that joins the circles, Meigle (6) has a scroll design on the joining band, Westland has circles at the edge of the joining band and Inchyra has notches.

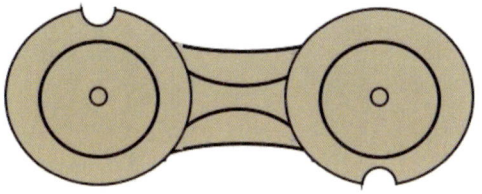

Inchyra Double Disc

The Double Disc symbols are a variant of the Z-Rod and Double Discs which could have been used to explain the structure of the Earth, planets and the celestial sphere beyond, the Sun and Moon and other paired items in harmony plus the Sun (as the planet) and Mithras (as the Invincible Sun) in balance.

Speculatively the order in which objects are explained to initiates could align with the Mithraic grades – the higher the grade the more was revealed.

Horseshoe / Arch

A general "arch" pattern can be seen in the symbols that have been given the Horseshoe and Arch names except for Rothiebrisbane, which has a somewhat distorted shape. 6 of the 18 objects are indistinct so 12 designs emerged. There is a wide range of detail within the general pattern from the simplicity of Sandness to the highly-decorated style of Crosskirk and the inclusion of concentric circles (as in the Z-Rod & Double Disc) at Strathpeffer.

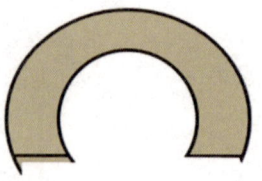

Sandness Horseshoe/Arch

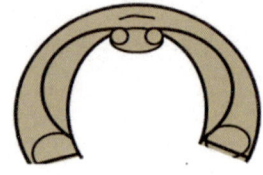

Crosskirk Horseshoe/Arch

Strathpeffer Horseshoe /Arch

The horseshoe and arch can be decoded (by taking the shape as an arc) as the arc of a planet's orbit, the entrance to a cave, the general shape of the inside of a Roman Mithraeum or the celestial sphere or, as with most of the symbols, all of these, perhaps others. Unlikely prospects include the "good luck" symbol, seemingly a superstition started when St Dunstan was a blacksmith in Canterbury (around 959) and the pre-Chaldean shape representing various moon goddesses – these cases are both outside the Pictish-Mithraism period.

The horseshoe and arch shapes can be recognised as representations of and from the indoor Mithraeum. "Of" the Mithraeum in the sense of its arched shape; "from" in the sense that within the Mithraeum there are representations of the celestial sphere etc.

Perhaps these decoded shapes were used instructionally to tell initiates about indoor Mithraea in which cult members would have met elsewhere and in the past but are not doing so in North East Scotland for reasons given above.

Decorated Rectangle

Of the 16 Decorated Rectangle objects 4 are indistinct and the example at Newton of Lewesk of a rectangle and crossed line is considered to be a later addition resulting in 11 individual designs being drawn.

This individuality itself underlines the difficulty in decoding what these symbols might mean, from the complexity of the Golspie object to the simplicity of the one at Grantown.

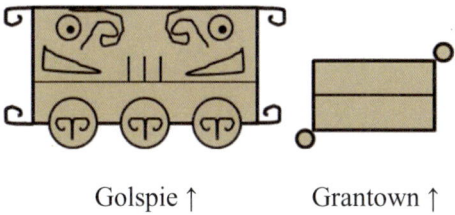

Golspie ↑   Grantown ↑

Some of these objects have elements of horizontal and / or vertical symmetry.

At this stage the author has no suggestions for a decode for these objects – they may just be decorative.

Notched Rectangle

There are 16 objects given this name of which 9 are superimposed with Z-Rods. 5 objects are indistinct – 11 separate designs emerged. There are no instances of the Z-Rod with Notched Rectangle variant and the Notched Rectangle alone on the same stone. For drawing simplicity and clarity, the Z-Rods are shown in the examples below with triangular terminals.

Almost all of these designs have cut -outs into the long sides of the shapes, even including the Westfield example shown here that does not have a Z-Rod across it. In contrast Cargill has neither Z-Rod nor cut-outs but maintains the general pattern of the longitudinal notch.

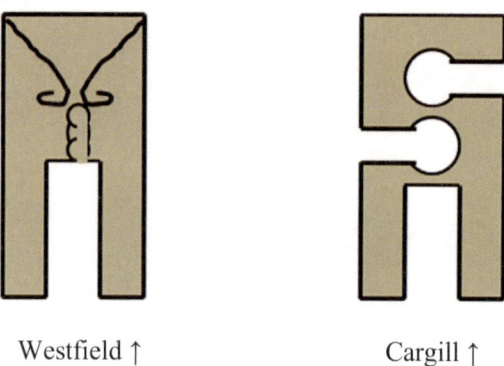

Westfield ↑   Cargill ↑

The Notched Rectangle shapes appear to represent the layout of an indoor Mithraeum typically having circle shaped cut-outs into the longitudinal sides. On the Raven Stone (Tyrie, Aberdeenshire) and Birnie Stone (near Elgin) the overall rectangular footprint has what could be construed as the "side benches" of a Mithraeum with statue niches (one on each side of the Mithraeum and near the Tauroctony end – possibly for Cautes and Cautopates).

The Maiden Stone, in Aberdeenshire, is almost identical to the Raven Stone footprint except the proximity of the cut-outs to the Tauroctony end is the opposite i.e. on the Raven Stone the left cut out or niche is nearer than the right and on the Maiden Stone the right niche is nearer than the left. The Tillypronie Stone is another variant on the theme – the niches are opposite one another; similar to the Inverallan Stone. The Ballintomb Stone has only one niche – in from the left and extending about two thirds of the way across the width of the rectangle.

Ardnilly is slightly different again, with semicircles cutting into the insides of the "side benches". There is a high correlation between the symbol stone rectangle symbols and the footprints of Mithraea such as in Ostia, Italy as shown in elsewhere in this publication. Ardnilly, Clynemilton and Tillypronie have semicircles on side benches suggesting a seat type indentation.

The interpretation of the Z-Rod shapes on Notched Rectangles is arguably the same as that for Z-Rods & Double Discs – the arrows are a drawing simplification of the "flames" which have been decoded as Cautes and Cautopates holding their torches to represent morning and night, the equinoxes etc. Additionally, these Z shapes could allude to Hydra linking Cancer and Capricorn.

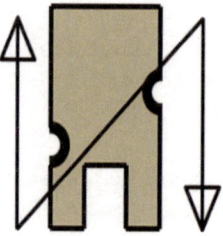

Maiden Stone Notched Rectangle with Z-Rod

Tyrie & Birnie Notched Rectangle with Z-Rod

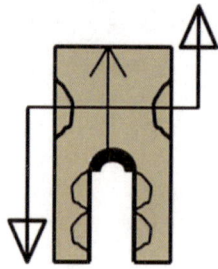

Tillypronie Notched Rectangle with Z-Rod

The Notched Rectangle shapes represent the shape and layout of a Roman Mithraeum, in some cases with indentations which equate to the niches which would have housed statues – typically Cautes and Cautopates. The addition of the Z-Rod in over half of these objects reinforces the presence of the statues of the torch bearers and could have been used to explain their importance in the mysteries of Mithras.

This is a very significant decode. This object is the only one on Pictish Stones that requires minimal decoding as it basically records the layout of the Roman Mithraeum and has acted as a key to the discovery that the Pictish Standing Stones were used as meeting places for people practising a version of Roman Mithraism. Not only would it have been a reminder to the "teacher" of the origin of Pictish-Mithraism but an excellent object for the initiate to be told about that origin plus enabling what could be revealed about the torch bearers.

Triple Disc

The Triple Disc is referred to as "cauldron" in some texts due to its shape and prospective use. 2 objects are indistinct and 12 designs emerged from the 13 items that were drawn. The result is 3 groups of objects with only the Monymusk Stone design not fitting any group.

Whilst a general pattern emerged, the 3 groups have distinct combinations of either smaller circles adjacent to the larger, central one, concentric circles (which look like rings) instead of the smaller circles and a horizontal line across the circles. The Monymusk example has decorations using circles and lines in the central portion. Collectively they do have the appearance of discs.

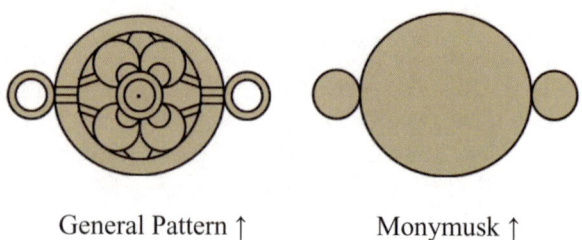

General Pattern ↑   Monymusk ↑

Cairnton, Tobar na Maor and Navidale (Group 1) follow the general pattern with the smaller circles horizontally on either side of the main circle but it has additional concentric circles; in the case of Cairnton there is a central dot in the main circle and dots slightly off-centre in the outer circles. These tend to echo the style of the Discs in the Z-Rod & Double Disc symbols and one might assume the associated meaning of Earth, planets and celestial sphere. In Group 2 the outer circles are replaced with rings and are on the vertical rather than horizontal axis. Each has a different interface to the main ring – from touching to what look like connecting links. The Dyce example has 3 concentric rings and a dot in the central circle. Group 3 has the horizontal line as its distinguishing feature; 4 of these symbols are of the central and side circle design with the 5th at Kintore (Churchyard) having outer rings and a line which has been drawn to represent what looks like a rod which together suggest a means of carrying. Here are 3 examples-

| Glamis | Inveravon (2) | Kintore |
| Manse | | Churchyard |

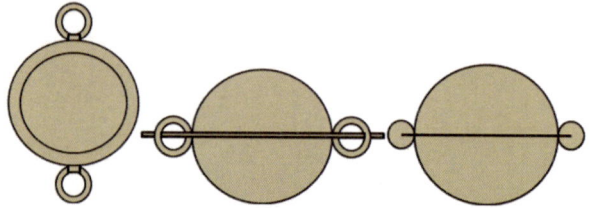

With its Triple Disc name a basically flat object is described. However, the alternative of "cauldron" suggests not only a three-dimensional depth but a practical function. It has also been termed krater, crater, vase and water container. Maybe within Mithraism these particular symbols have several meanings. Each component of the Tauroctony has a constellation / celestial counterpart: Bull – Taurus; Dog – Canis Minor & Canis Major; Snake – Hydra, Serpens, Draco; Raven – Corvus; Scorpion – Scorpius; Wheat ears on bull's tail – Spica; Cautes & Cautopates – Gemini; Lion – Leo; Crater (cup) – Crater; Sol – Sun; Luna – Moon; Cave – Universe.

So Crater or Cup appears with this Mithraic context. A small beaker is associated with the Corax Mithraic Grade; in the Nymphus Mithraic Grade rite, Venus can be offered a cup of water; a libation bowl is associated with the Pater Mithraic Grade. Apparently part of the Roman Mithraic ritual when progressing through the grades involved water. Water is one of the four elements with air, fire and Earth. Many of the Pictish Symbol Stones are in close proximity to water, generally rivers.

Whilst cauldron, libation bowl, water, plus rings and rods as means of carrying could be contenders in this decode, the greater likelihood is perhaps something more esoteric than obvious. Multiple meanings such as Mithraic grades, water as an element etc. are not discounted. However, with the symbol stones revealing the principles of the mysteries of Mithras and some limited recording of the indoor Mithraeum a pointer for decoding the Triple Discs lies in the paintings and statuary that would have been seen in Mithraea. With the addition of decodes for other symbols plus a deconstruct of the symbol into its components there are a central circle – the celestial Sphere / constellations /

zodiac – and smaller circles that are 180° apart. In Group 3 these components are linked together with a straight line ("rod"). In Group 2 the Glamis Manse (1), Aberlemno (Church) and Kintradwell (1) designs can be seen as having an outer ring – the zodiac. Cairnton in Group 1 has the concentric ring elements similar to those in the Z-Rod & Double Disc.

As Pictish Symbols tend to complement one another and collectively conceal but also reveal a religious belief, the Triple Disc decode can be unravelled despite the incised circles being difficult to decipher as the infill remains in place.

Complementing other key Mithraic symbols on the Pictish Stones, the Triple Disc represents the zodiac with Cancer and Capricorn constellations (the gates from and to Heaven) 180° apart. They coincide with the summer and winter solstices.

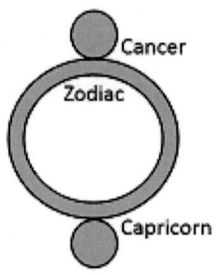

Tuning Fork

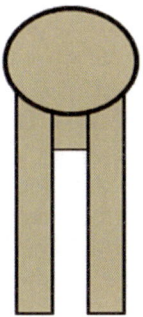

Although there are similarities, these "Tuning Forks" are categorised as a separate design to Decorated and Notched Rectangles. There are 11 of these objects, 1 is indistinct and 9 designs emerged which have been arranged into 3 groups, the third of which has partially intact examples with only the parallel line parts of the object visible. The other two groups follow a broad, general pattern. The adherence to a general pattern is much less in this symbol than in several others. This suggests a framework design either with the sculptors' interpretation in adding decoration or, indeed, misinterpretation. Overall, however, the concept of a rounded shape at the top connected to two broad, parallel lines has been achieved. Group 1 has either a completed oval or round shape at the top of the symbol. Group 2 has a variety of semi-circular type shapes on top of the parallel lines.

The decode for the Notched Rectangle is that its shape represents the shape and layout of a Roman Mithraeum. The tuning fork is generally not dissimilar but has neither indentations nor is it ever crossed with a Z-Rod. The broad, parallel lines are like the lower part of the Notched Rectangle design so they could equate to the benches of a Mithraeum.

The Pictish Symbol Stone symbols are carved in a two-dimensional fashion without any clear attempts to suggest a three-dimensional projection (except for the "waist" effect used with the Z-Rod & Double Disc) or a suggestion that part of the carving may be "coming out" of the slab. The Tuning Fork may be the exception. If the parallel lines are indeed representative of the "side benches" of a Roman Mithraeum, then the shape at the top of them could be at right angles to the benches. The view into an Indoor Mithraeum would have been of two benches and the Tauroctony scene at the opposite end. The curved shape of the top of the Tuning Fork would be like the curved shape of the roof of the Mithraeum.

The decode for the Tuning Fork is that it symbolises a view into a Roman Mithraeum with parallel side benches leading towards the Tauroctony scene whilst alluding to the curved roof of an Indoor Mithraeum. This symbol would have enabled a teacher to describe the inside of a Mithraeum and is a simplified version of the Notched Rectangle in that it does not contain any iconography of the Mysteries of Mithras as such.

Symbol Groups & Stone Groups

The symbols on stones cannot be considered to be randomly distributed. Several have the V-Rod & Crescent and Z-Rod & Double Disc juxtaposed on the same stone surface and this suggests some composite meaning or maybe a direct progression in revealing a meaning or meanings from one to the next. Conversely, the lower than expected presence of the V-Rod & Crescent and higher than expected presence of the Z-Rod & Double Disc on the early stones in the geographic areas explored in Chapter 8 (The Start of Pictish-Mithraism) tends to suggest that one stone design could be used to explain aspects of another's meaning as well as its own.

At minimum, in the context of Pictish-Mithraism, some typical symbol groups show the Enticement (in the V-Rod), the explanation of Mithras, Cautes and Cautopates (in the Z-Rod) and one Mithraic Grade (Nymphus in the case of the Mirror symbols). Examples of groups of two are the Brandsbutt Stone, Aberdeenshire; Elgin Cathedral; Aberlemno: and of three are the Picardy Stone, Insch; Clach Ard, Skye.

Considering the decodes above, there is arguably a "minimum set" of symbols needed to explain the principles of Pictish-Mithraism – shown in this picture:

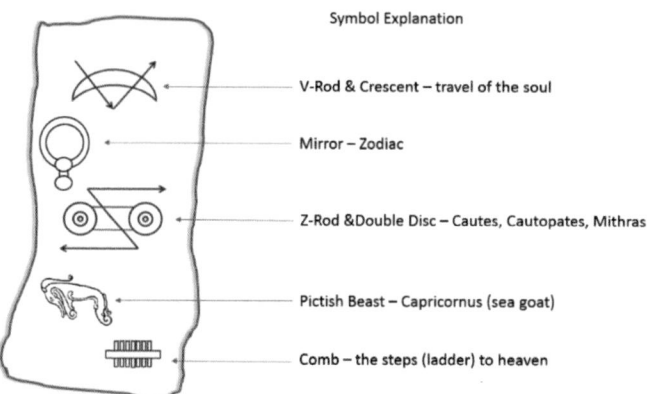

Hypothetical "Class 1" Stone – Top 5 Essential Symbols

Symbol Explanation

V-Rod & Crescent – travel of the soul

Mirror – Zodiac

Z-Rod & Double Disc – Cautes, Cautopates, Mithras

Pictish Beast – Capricornus (sea goat)

Comb – the steps (ladder) to heaven

These symbols could be incorporated in a single stone, a set of adjacent stones or a collection of stones in geographic proximity. These, together with other Mithraic symbols, could be used to take initiates through the Mithraic Grades; maybe some stones were used specifically for, say, higher ladder grades only.

This notion of "grouping" is not dissimilar to the relationship of Christian parish churches to cathedrals.

Stones are clustered in many areas, for example Glamis / Eassie / Tealing / Wester Denoon / Kirriemuir; Craigton / Dunrobin / Golspie; Brandsbutt / Kintore / Drimmies / East Balhaggardy /Logie Elphinstone; Knocknagael / Lochardil / Torgorm.

Missing Items

It is known that in Roman Mithraism the central statue was the Tauroctony. Explanations can be given to the Pictish Mithraic iconography linked back to Roman Mithraism but some expected items are missing. For example, the Tauroctony itself – although some components such as the snake (or serpent) and, of course, Cautes and Cautopates (depicted as the arrows in Z-Rods) have been carved. The only zodiac sign so far identified on the symbol stones is the Pictish Beast representing Capricorn but perhaps the skywards part of the Open Air Mithraeum is enough. Tauroctonies also have wind gods but Zephyrus, Boreas, Notus and Eurus are absent too – maybe when a belief follower is outside there are other ways of explaining these. What is more likely is that Pictish-Mithraism as a derivative of Roman Mithraism transitioned into a religious belief that did not have, or need to have, all the features of its predecessor. This is most likely just as the earliest version of Mithraism with Mithra as a Persian God changed when it transitioned into an Indian God within Vedic Hinduism.

Non-Mithraic Objects

Objects within the following categories are commented on in "Non-Mithraic Objects – Identified & Recorded" at www.pictish-mithraism.com :

Fantastic Beast / Creature	People	Rounded Shape
Crosses	Animal	Angular Shape
Bird	Script	Fish
Plant	Implement, device	Angel
Biblical Story	Cup Marking	Bosses

7
STONES & DISTANT VIEWS – THE "OPEN AIR" MITHRAEUM

There are two components to the Open Air Mithraeum 1) terrestrial and 2) "as far as the eye can see".

Having decoded the symbols in the context of Mithraism a significant step is realised in how the religious belief was practiced. They are carved on the symbol stones providing the basic principles of Roman Mithraism and a record of the layout of the indoor Mithraeum. These act as a reminder for the existing cult followers and as a means of educating an initiate. The stones become the terrestrial part of the Open Air Mithraeum.

What "the eye can see" ranges from flora, fauna, fields, rivers, the sea, mountains, the sky and what can be seen in the sky – planets, constellations, the zodiac etc. The indoor Mithraeum's representation of planets and constellations typically painted on ceilings or walls is not required – they can be seen in the outdoor version but astronomical and astrological knowledge would be needed to identify them.

Representation of Enticement, Tauroctony and Initiation Grades plus the inclusion of associated local customs / cults / religions or forms of adaptation, absorption or recognition (Mithraism with or to other religious beliefs and/or vice versa) would be a start point in designing the terrestrial part of an Open Air Mithraeum – beyond just randomly placing the Pictish Symbols. The adaptation category (taking one symbol and modifying it to become another) would be the least straightforward to decode requiring a knowledge of both Mithraism and the local item. However, indoor Mithraea did contain more than the Mithraic grouping (Mithras, Tauroctony, his companions) but also other gods that were revered at the time of the Roman Empire plus, in some locations, Celtic deities and what started as very specific local cults such as that of the Dacian or Danubian Riders (followed in the area of modern day Romania) but which spread within the Roman Empire.

Constituents could, therefore, include:

Enticement – attracting a target audience, such as the military, to prospects of life after death, a hereafter, gaining "secret" knowledge etc.

Tauroctony – Mithras himself (or a representation of what Mithras stands for); animals – dog, snake, scorpion (or a representation of them in "sky" terms or otherwise); the zodiac & constellations (seen in the sky) but maybe needing a form of pointer and most certainly an explanation; Mithras's companions (or what they represent); water container; bull; knife; winds; elements (earth, wind, fire, air) etc.

Grades – planets (visible in the sky) but again maybe needing a form of pointer; grade names (raven, male bride, soldier, lion, Persian, courier of the sun, father) and their related symbols.

Local customs / cults / religions – Celtic gods; symbols of local customs; non-Mithraic symbols etc.

Considering the skywards view, on a clear day the Sun is the most visible planet (it was considered to be a planet in the time frame of Roman Mithraism) followed by the Moon (also considered to be a planet) then, on occasion, other planets (such as Venus) and brighter stars. During a clear night the planets, the zodiac and a much wider set of stars is visible – in fact, broadly a hemisphere of the universe. This sky component can replace much of the iconography of the indoor Mithraeum quite simply as it is not needed. In the night sky the relevant Constellations can be seen – dependent on the time of year. Any star (indeed galaxy) forms, otherwise represented in the indoor Mithraeum – including the Milky Way – can be seen by the observer on Earth.

Therefore, in designing the terrestrial part of the Open Air Mithraeum there is no need to include the planets and stars as such – maybe just their relationship within the mystery and/or as locational pointers. An icon may not be needed when the real thing is visible.

However, there may be aspects of the view skywards, otherwise depicted but obscured in the Mithraeum, which are visible to anyone (Mithraist or not) that in the context of Mithraism need to be further obscured. The carved symbols might then need to obscure something that may be deduced directly from looking at the sky or, conversely, stone based symbols could rely on the sky view to complete the symbol. Nothing should be obvious to the uninitiated. Furthermore, a stone based symbol could be used as an indicator to use part of the sky view to decode the symbol or, simply, to be a pointer.

If the intent is to mimic the indoor Mithraeum then replication of layout, orientation and location is necessary. Some of the indoor Mithraea seem to have a specific East/West orientation; good examples are those in Ostia, Italy. The Tauroctony is at the east end; the inbuilt benches are set on the north side facing south and the South side facing north; the entrance is at the west end so anyone entering faces towards the Tauroctony. All this gives orientation along the Earth's north-south axis and facilitates observing where the Sun and Moon rise and set, plus gives a reference point for the equinox and solstice locations.

Indoor Mithraea are located close to running water – partly, probably, for practical purposes but maybe to ensure all elements are present and visible – earth, air, fire and water. Fire can be created by lighting candles for example. Outdoor versions could readily be erected near running water with fire being represented by a view of the sun or by burning objects.

In some places several Mithraea are built in close proximity to one another – maybe providing different but complementary functions. Again this could be achieved, if wished, with the Open Air Mithraeum.

Here are two examples of the terrestrial parts of "Open Air" Mithraea:
These photographs are not to the same scale.

Broomend of Crichie, Inverurie
Attribution – Debra Burris www.occc.edu

Aberlemno 2, Angus
Attribution – Catfish Jim en.wikipedia

On a clear, frosty night the skywards view would have contained planets and stars. To those "in the know" it would have been possible to identify specific planets, constellations and the Milky Way.

By considering some Class 1 and 2 symbol stones we can see that:

The stones were used for "religious" purposes. Latterly Christian and initially for another religious belief.
The initial religious belief comes from Roman Mithraism, the symbols are representative of that mystery cult and can be traced to an interpretation of what is seen in Roman Mithraea.

There was tolerance for specific religious beliefs, adaptation and adoption of pre-existing beliefs and transition to newer beliefs e.g. to Christianity.

Original locations can have particular significance e.g. distant views, closeness to rivers etc.

Some of the locations may have had the equivalent of the Christian "cathedral" functionality.

Two examples are here. A further eight are in Appendix 1 – "Case Studies"

Aberlemno Stones – south of the Mounth with both Class 1 and 2 stones – are located in the Brechin / Forfar area at RCAHMS site numbers NO55NW 8, 26 & 33.

Together the three sites at Aberlemno (three stones by the roadside at Crosstoun, one in the churchyard and one at nearby Flemington Farm) and nearby Woodwrae have Class 1 and 2 stones covering many of this section's selected features (Dyce and Strathmartine appear to be the only other locations with both Class 1 and 2 stones). Features are variously church location, near a river, open views, biblical story, a range of symbol designs, people, animals, fantastic beasts and the possibility of the equivalent of a "cathedral" type setting. Woodwrae is included with this Aberlemno grouping as it is thought the stone is from the Aberlemno location.

The Class 2 church yard stone has on one side a Latin cross surrounded by beasts with exaggerated claws, Hippocamps and other creatures. The intertwined animals are in a style similar to that found in door frames to some church doors in Norway around 1000 CE (cast copy examples are in the Victoria and Albert Museum, London).

The reverse has at its top a Z-Rod and Notched Rectangle adjacent to a Triple Disc symbol with an extensive battle scene below – supposedly recording the 685 CE Battle of Dunnichen. This face of the stone is laid out in registers with a "one- off" scene in the lower right of a foot soldier being attacked by what appears to be a crow / raven.

At the top of the church yard stone is a Z-Rod with Notched Rectangle (this is one of the simplest of the nine examples identified so far) which represents the same elements as the more numerous Z-Rod and Double Disc i.e. the flame-like rods. However, the flame directions are different from the other eight examples. Compared with the Z-Rod orientation when with Double Discs, the rods here are rotated ninety degrees counter-clockwise. Moving to the interpretation – the rods represent Cautes and Cautopates and their torches; in the morning or spring equinox there would typically be an upward flaming torch and in the evening or autumn equinox a downward extinguishing torch.

The Notched Rectangle represents the Roman Mithraeum with side benches and end wall which typically housed the Tauroctony. These combined symbols are reminiscent of the practising of the Mysteries of Mithras within an enclosed (often underground) Mithraeum – for Pictish-Mithraism the enclosed, or indoor, Mithraeum is replaced by the Open Air Mithraeum. This symbolism could be instructional as to the origins of Pictish-Mithraism and the practice of Roman Mithraism in a Mithraeum. Perhaps placing this object at the top of the stone has some significance in that the viewer looks skyward – perhaps expanding the symbolism of the Z to indicate the travel of the soul which would typically be shown by the arrows in the V-Rod & Crescent.

Adjacent to the Z-Rod and Notched Rectangle is the Triple Disc – in general pattern (there are 15 of these objects) a large circle with two small circles on either side of a central axis. Kintradwell, near Brora has an almost identical example which also looks like a water container with a form of carrying ring on each side. Water and proximity to water are important in Roman Mithraism and this attribute may have been brought forward into Pictish-Mithraism. However, placing this symbol at the top of the stone would enable a prompt to look for the zodiac and Capricorn in the night sky – the decode for this symbol is in Chapter 6 (Mithraic Symbols – Identified and Decoded).

Variations of the so-called sea horse – the Hippocamp – are rare on Pictish Symbol Stones and only seen on Cross Stones. The Aberlemno carving is very clear as a pair of intertwined beasts with front legs, manes and fish-like or dolphin-like tails. Its meaning relative to standing stones is unclear. Although not dissimilar to the "sea-goat" or Capricorn (the decode for the Pictish Beast) there is no apparent Pictish-Mithraism context when displayed in this intertwine.

Just above the tails is a Triquetra with flat rather than rounded sides. The symbol has ancient Germanic and Celtic art use as well as in Christianity from early time to the current day. Its use on this stone and at St Vigeans and Meigle Class 2 stones is probably Christian as it is not seen on Class 1 stones.

The setting for the roadside stones is high open land with long distance views in all directions – to the north is the River South Esk. In the vicinity are the remains of a cairn, cist and fort.

Of the two Class 1 roadside stones the circles incised on one are basically indecipherable. The other stone has four symbols on one side with cup marks low down on the other.

With an elongated Latin Cross surrounded by bosses at its arms then a Celtic style circle, the Class 2 stone is enhanced with angels holding books on the Cross side and a biblical connection on the reverse – a representation of David pulling apart the jaws of a lion. Like the Class 2 stone in the church yard, this is also arranged in registers on the reverse.

Alongside the biblical scene is a centaur carrying what looks like an axe over his shoulder and perhaps a tree. The middle section is a hunting scene with trumpeters (itself in a three register layout) surmounted by a Z-Rod with Double Discs and a V-Rod with ornate Crescent.

Looking skywards then down to the back of the roadside Class 2 stone, one's gaze drops firstly onto the V-Rod and Crescent then the Z-Rod and Double Disc. Compared with many, these are rather ornate with the carver taking the pattern used on the Cross side to infill the Crescent. In Pictish-Mithraism decoding the V comprises two arrows (one taking the soul from beyond the celestial sphere at birth, the other returning it at death) with the Crescent primarily being the view to the sky. The direction of the arrows is suggested by the flame designs as used in all the Z-Rod and Double Disc objects. 20 instances of the V-Rod & Crescent are at the top of Class 1 stones – appropriate positioning for explaining one of the fundamental principles of Mithraism – here carried onto a "transition" stone and no less appropriate in a Christian explanation of "Heaven".

For Pictish-Mithraism the Z-Rod and Double Disc have been decoded as:

the upper, right facing, rod signifying morning and the spring equinox (the torch held by Cautes),

the lower, left facing, rod as evening and the autumn equinox (the torch held by Cautopates),

the connecting rod being Mithras (connecting together the day, the months between equinoxes and time itself),

the discs being multi-depiction with Mithras as Sol Invictus and the Sun (sol) in balance plus being the Moon and Sun in harmony or tension plus representing the components of the universe – the Earth at the centre, the planets and the celestial sphere. More importantly, in the majority of instances of this symbol, the three-dimensional view suggested by the "waist" effect of the lines between the discs represents a contained universe – Heaven is beyond that material universe. This Aberlemno example is unusual as the lines joining the discs are parallel – maybe the carver had space limitations as the rod connecting the Z Rods themselves is short so the usual position for the "waist" effect lines is not available.

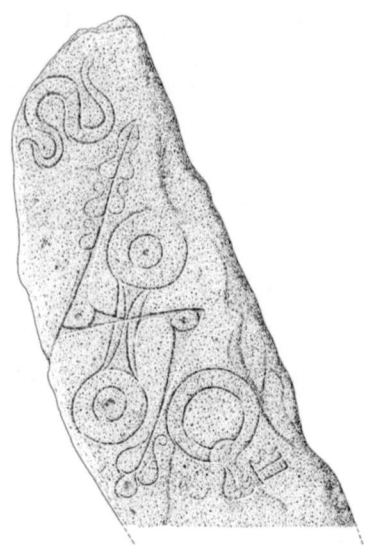

Again looking skywards then down, this time from the front of the roadside Class 1 stone, one sees a serpent then the Z-Rod and Double Disc that dominate this stone (complete with three concentric circles in the "double disc" part – the Earth, planets and celestial sphere plus the "waist" effect giving a three-dimensional depth) followed by the Mirror and alongside it a Comb.

The Mirror – the second most numerous symbol on the stones – is in Pictish-Mithraism decoding a representation of the zodiac (here as a very clear ring) connected to a Double Disc with the overlap point arguably being Capricorn. A Knockando / Pulvrenan Stone has a similar layout except the centre is dominated by a weathered flower type symbol. The reverse of this Aberlemno Stone has cup marks low down.

The layout of the symbols and the size and dominance of the Z-Rod & Double Disc may have been prompted by the shape of the stone – which may have originally have been vertical.

This example of the Comb appears to have 7lines. The number 7 has important significance in Roman Mithraism. The modern day planets known at the time were Jupiter, Mars, Venus, Mercury and Saturn but were combined with the Sun and Moon to give the, then, 7 known "planets". These 7 planets are associated with the 7 steps in the ladder of initiation grades in the Roman Mithraic cult.

Looking back up to the Serpent there is arguably a linkage between the symbol on the stone and the sky, particularly night sky, views above it. The serpent in the context of the constellations can be Hydra, Serpens or Draco. Hydra as one of the 88 modern constellations stretches from Libra to Canis Minor (over 90° of the Celestial Sphere) but in the period when the equinoxes were in Taurus and Scorpio – Mithraic implications – Hydra was considered to extend further by including Sextans, Crater and Corvus (more like 180°). Perhaps the serpent symbol is used to explain part of the Mysteries of Mithras such as the serpent's head beyond the 7 planets so at the eighth gate, the celestial sphere, reaching into Heaven. It also represents eternal time.

Nearby at Flemington Farm a Class 1 stone was ploughed up in the early 1960s. The layout of the Horseshoe / Arch and Pictish Beast is the same as the Bruceton Stone about 20 miles away.

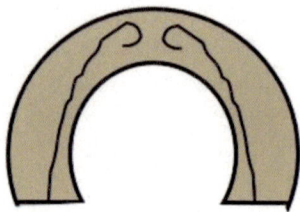

The Arch is the view into the Roman Mithraeum with its tunnel type shape and the Arch is also the shape at the so-called Tauroctony end which would have housed the Tauroctony statue.

It could also represent the skyward view to the zodiac.

The Pictish Beast is decoded as the "sea goat" which is Capricorn – astrologically the Gate of the Gods through which the soul travels on death into immortality. In Pictish-Mithraism, the connection between the V-Rod & Crescent, the Mirror and the Pictish Beast Symbols is Capricorn. On a symbol stone the Pictish beast could act as a "pointer" to the Capricorn constellation and, with reference to the V-Rod & Crescent, enable an explanation of the soul's travel via the celestial sphere back to Heaven, and immortality, on death.

When Woodwrae Castle (just west of Aberlemno) was demolished in the early 1800s a stone was found that had been used for flooring. Central parts of the Cross seem to have been chiselled away and areas of the relief carvings on the reverse have been removed – predominantly, it seems, of the hunting scene. However, some unusual and "one-off" carvings remain.

On the reverse at Woodwrae are a bull (only one of two carvings known beyond Burghead), a Double Disc (the only one known with peripheral concentric circles), a hunting scene with two dogs or hounds (one looks as if it is attacking a large animal) and what looks like the remains of an L-shaped Rectangle.

On the Cross side there are five carvings of Beasts with Exaggerated Claws, Interlaced Animals, a beast with human legs in its mouth and a beast carrying some prey. The significance of these in Christian theology terms is not yet known – there is no arguable Pictish-Mithraism relevance.

And finally for Aberlemno, perhaps the stones at the church, Flemington Farm and the one once located at Woodwrae Castle were erected with the others at the roadside (bearing in mind that this may well have been just a track – maybe just for access to the stone site).

Tillytarmont Stones – north of the Mounth with Class 1 stones – are located in the Keith / Huntly area at RCAHMS site numbers NJ54NW 1, 11, 20 & 22.

From open farmland at the confluence of two rivers 5 stones have been discovered, mainly through ploughing activity, over a one-hundred-year period. Collectively they have a selection of the more numerous Mithraic symbols.

All of the "top five" Class 1 symbol stone figures across what is now Scotland are represented here – the V-rod & Crescent (twice), Mirror (twice), the Z-Rod & Double Disc (twice), Pictish Beast and Comb. Additionally, there is an example of a Mirror Case, a Horseshoe / Arch, an Eagle and a Goose – giving the name "Goose Stone" to one of the first stones discovered here – and an unusual Z-Rod with Serpent. With finds appearing from the 1860s to 1970s maybe there are more stones in this location which could further lead to the speculation about the importance of this site. Elsewhere in this publication the idea of the equivalent of a "cathedral" has been mentioned with other prospective locations being Rhynie, Aberlemno and St Vigeans. With the piece of land where all the stones were discovered being a relatively narrow strip at the confluence of the Rivers Isla and Deveron the "cathedral" prospect is maybe further enhanced as water appears to be of significance in Pictish-Mithraism.

An Eagle is not uncommon (of the twenty-two bird objects on stones, sixteen are Eagles) but there are only three other examples of a Goose. Maybe the Goose links into some Celtic form of belief and worship – it can be associated with aggression in Celtic mythology and as symbolising the Holy Spirit in the Celtic Church. The Eagle has been seen variously as a symbol of power, the noon day sun, a messenger, eternal life etc. – no specific options for association with Pictish-Mithraism but perhaps an acceptance of positioning Pictish-Mithraism symbols alongside those of a pre-existing religious belief; potentially transition.

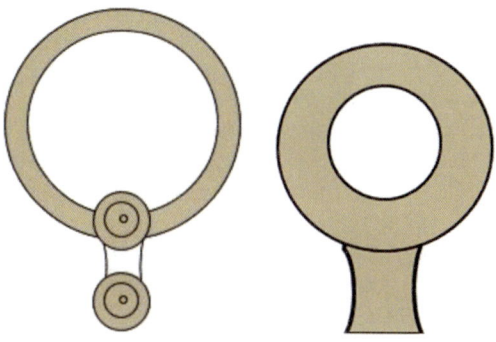

Maybe the apparent difference between the two Mirrors (drawn on pages 22 and 23 of Appendix A on the website) is due to incising tools and techniques rather than portraying a different meaning.

Often in standing stone books the Mirror and Mirror Case are described as complementary – hence their names. However, for Pictish-Mithraism interpretation this is inapplicable – they are neither mirror, nor mirror case but it is convenient to use these terms.

The Group 1 examples of the Mirror in Pictish-Mithraism decoding comprise the Double Disc part of the Z-Rod & Double Disc design with the larger circle being the zodiac. The Tillytarmont example also has the three concentric circles in the Double Disc part – these are the Earth, planets and celestial sphere.

The Mirror Case represents the birth of Mithras (the lower part of the design being the birth from the rock) and also his holding the zodiac (i.e. the circle shape).

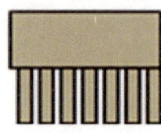

The Tillytarmont design of the Comb has 7 "teeth". Only one other example of this symbol type has 7 "teeth" on one side of a central bar i.e. Collace, near Coupar Angus. A Comb at Inveravon, Speyside has 7 "teeth" on each side of a central bar. The number 7has important significance in Roman Mithraism. The planets know at the time were Jupiter, Mars, Venus, Mercury and Saturn. Combined with the Sun and Moon the 7 "planets" are associated with the 7 steps in the ladder of initiation grades in the Roman Mithraic cult.

The Pictish Beast – the sea-goat as Capricorn – is also present on a Tillytarmont Stone. Its interpretation complements the V-Rod & Crescent and Mirror at this site in enabling the gateway through the celestial sphere to Heaven beyond to be explained.

Of the Z-Rod and Double Disc symbols the one discovered in 1944 (known as Stone 2) has the usual three concentric circles (drawn at Appendix A page 34 on the website) compared with the indistinct Stone 3 discovered in 1867 and refound in 1954 with only two concentric circles. Both provide the same message of Cautes and Cautopates linked together by Mithras with the associated symbolism of morning and evening, spring and autumn plus the Double Discs having several meanings, such as the Earth in the centre with the planets then the celestial sphere, the Sun and Moon paired in harmony and/or the Sun and Mithras in balance.

Z-Rods with Serpents are unusual – there are only six of the type of design as at Tillytarmont. Taking the Z-Rod to represent Cautes and Cautopates connected together by Mithras the Double Discs are replaced by the Serpent which can be interpreted as a single constellation, a set of constellations which stretch across about half of the zodiac, time itself, eternal life etc. In Pictish-Mithraism terms this arguably reinforces the connectivity and all-embracing position of Mithras.

With this selection of symbols concentrated in a small space and located between two rivers, the case for Tillytarmont having a purpose well beyond that of a stand-alone symbol stone is strong; in other words, the equivalent of "cathedral". If all the stones stood together at the same time, there would have been an opportunity to introduce the basics of the Mysteries of Mithras through to more esoteric aspects by progression through the grades.

8
THE START OF PICTISH-MITHRAISM WHO, WHEN AND WHERE?

Having discovered that the symbols on the Pictish Symbol Stones represent aspects of a form of Mithraism and that Roman Mithraism was practised close to Pictland by Hadrian's Wall, then a contender for introducing a form of Mithraism must be people associated with the Roman Army. This sets a time frame between the first and fifth centuries CE. But who are the people – were they soldiers, auxiliaries, tradespeople or others who had learned about Mithraism?

This publication is concerned with Pictland being the location of the symbol stones. However, the stones range in location from the Orkney Islands to the Outer Hebrides, the North East of Scotland up to Caithness and down to Fife. In amongst this wide area stones with their symbols would surely have started somewhere specific then spread out, rather than rapidly appearing across many places. A challenge is finding that initial "somewhere".

Who? Perhaps the builders and worshippers were one and the same people; conversely, maybe the builders of the stones were different from those who used them. Someone had to cause them to be built; someone had to organise their planning and creation. There are questions of timing – when were they built; and timescale – over what period were they used? This is explored in detail at www.pictish-mithraism.com.

For our purposes, builders are the people who carved and erected the stones (or took existing standing stones and carved onto them). A great part of the "intrigue" is why, when these are called Pictish Standing Stones, was there seemingly such a gap between when the Picts were named Picts (late 3rd Century CE) and the first stones historically being dated as around the 4th / 5th Century CE? Were they created by the Picts (arguably a big assumption) or others? Someone with visual knowledge of what we now know as the Pictish Symbols and with the ability to carve in stone must have been the builder. What is carved must be quite clear and there probably was some order to the layout. This tends to suggest someone (singular and plural) with existing skills rather than self-taught. At the time the people with such skills were not within Pictland – to date there is no suitable archaeological evidence of similarly carved items – so they must have been incomers. The nearest would have been in the vicinity of Hadrian's Wall (at the time the Antonine wall was either unmanned or scarcely manned). There is physical evidence that carving skills had been employed there – not least for Mithraea. Perhaps the source of the carvers was the Roman army or its associated trades people. Not only would the carvers have had the carving skills, they most likely would have seen the Mithraea at first hand.

We need to consider who it was that caused the designs to be created and carved. Probably that can be ascribed to the worshippers, the ones who wanted to keep the religious belief alive and extend its following. But who were they? Because of the Mithraic connection with the Pictish Symbols it is reasonable to assume the connection is with Mithraea. Some possibilities about the builders and worshippers are that they:
1) came from around Hadrian's Wall (Roman army or otherwise),

2) were local people in Pictland with a Roman Army genealogy,
3) were local people who had seen Mithraea in Britannia or in Europe, or
4) were from Roman establishments that had existed in Pictland.

It should be remembered that the Roman army "pensioned off" its soldiers (probably also auxiliaries). Part of the pensioning off was the opportunity to remain at an outpost which for someone out-posted for a long period might well equate to contentedly remaining in situ. This opens up several prospects for the ethnicity of potential builders and worshippers – they could be from other parts of the Roman Empire (conquered and otherwise) but residing in Britain, "British" people who had become accustomed to the Roman customs and adopting them (including their religions) or merchants and traders maintaining an import base in Britain. Contrary to what in the past has been gleaned at school, the Romans were not necessarily from Rome. In fact, the British region was at times administered from other than Rome, for example from Trier in, then, Belgic Gaul.

The Roman regime, in common with the Persian ones in the first half millennium BCE, had a habit of taking people from "pacified" acquisitions, placing them in their armies then dispatching them to other parts of the empire or potential expanded empire. So the prospect for people coming from places well remote from Pictland is high – and they could have come with their religious belief or a susceptibility to one that they might be sympathetic towards.

Looking at monuments from around Hadrian's Wall there are indications of the nationality or homeland of some of the dedicators, such as Asturian from North Spain; Tungrian from the Western Ardennes; Pannonians from a territory of the present day western part of Hungary with parts in Austria, Croatia, Serbia, Slovenia, Slovakia and

Bosnia & Herzegovina (basically bounded on two sides by the river Danube); Dalmatian from what is now Croatia and parts of Bosnia & Herzegovina; Batavian from The Netherlands; Frisian from coastal parts of The Netherlands, Denmark and Germany; Nervian from inland parts of Belgium; Brixian from Northern Italy and more. So the Roman Army genealogy from this evidence alone is very broad. Valeria Victrix, the Roman XX (20th) Legion had been posted to several parts of what is now Britain, including Hadrian's Wall.

The conclusion is the demonstration above of a sound argument for a Roman Army connection for the initial builders of the symbol stones and the worshippers of a form of Mithraism.

When? To establish timing, the next step is to consider where the Roman Army either had a presence in Pictland or where its personnel (or ex-personnel) might have settled then to narrow down towards a prospective start period for Pictish-Mithraism.

Roman Army presence and influence was in several periods. In AD 80 Agricola, as Governor of Britannia, advanced to the River Tay building Inchtuthil Camp across the Tay in 82 and in 83 engaged with the local population in the battle of Mons Graupius.

The Gask Ridge and Glen Blocker establishments were constructed around 86/87 and the Antonine Wall between 142 and 154. Septimius Severus campaigned north of the River Forth between 208 and 210. In 306 Chlorus prosecuted war against the Picts. Their final withdrawal from Britannia was 410.

Within this 330-year timeframe there are a number of enablers and limits to when a form of Mithraism could have been introduced. Enablers include the physical presence within Pictland of Mithraic believers (worshippers) and the opportunity to set up Mithraea. A time of conflict would limit, probably exclude, activity. This would eliminate Agricola's campaign culminating, for Pictland anyway, in the battle of Mons Graupius. From that period walls with military presence were in use from 142 to 162 – the Antonine Wall – and, more distant, from 122 to 138 then 164 to 401 – Hadrian's Wall. In addition, there were Gask Ridge and Glen Blocker establishments so collectively a controlling presence from 71 to 213. However, the nature of the walls could at times have been to regulate the movement of people, collect taxes etc. It is suggested that in the vicinity of Hadrian's Wall there were local settlements and seemingly some evidence of Roman personnel in a family life with members of the local population. Key limiters would have been times of military strife.

Prevalent belief at any given time would also have had an enabler / limit effect. Pictish Symbol Stones have not only coded Mithraic Symbols and, to us, clear Christian significance (Crosses, Bible stories etc.) but also objects most likely from other beliefs (such as salmon mystically revered as it can live in both fresh and salt water). With Mithraea appearing by Hadrian's Wall – Rudchester and Carrawburgh supposedly founded in the early 3rd century – this tends to set an opening window for Mithraism extending northwards in Britannia. Emperor Constantine's favour ceased to be with the Mithraists following the battle at the Milvian Bridge in 312 CE.

Initially the toleration of Christian with other beliefs – the edict of Milan in 313 CE – followed by the adoption of Christianity as the state religion – by Theodosius 1 in 391 –

would have set progressively stronger closing windows for Roman Mithraism.

Roman withdrawal from Britannia could have given some Army personnel the chance to remain in the country. They could have retained their religious belief with them whilst continuing to settle in their existing location (e.g. Roman Army; more precisely ex-Roman Army) or relocating. Two specific dates would qualify – the withdrawal from Britannia about 400 to final withdrawal in 410 and the withdrawal from Pictland around 212. These would have given two timelines for the pursuit of Pictish-Mithraism. The longer one, timeline 1 below, stretching from the early 200s and the shorter, timeline 2, from the early 400s.

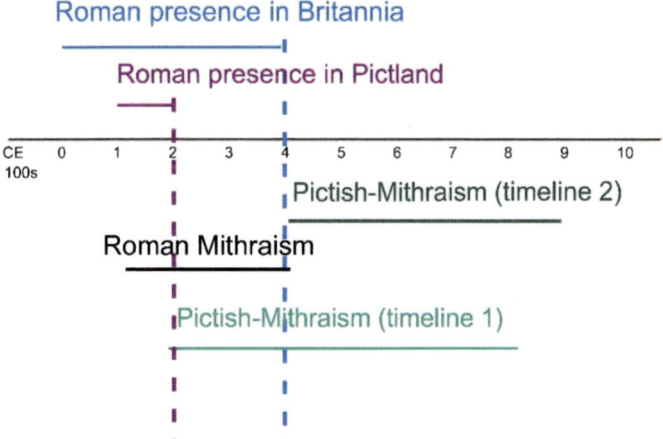

As we are considering an ensuing form of Roman Mithraism the 212 date is favourable as it is in the time period of the setting up of Mithraea by Hadrian's Wall (with a positive assumption about the popularity of the religious belief). Also, pursuing Mithraism seems to have been encouraged by Roman emperors; particularly, in this period, by Commodus (180 to 192), Septimius Severus (193 to 211) and Caracalla (211 to 217).

The post- final withdrawal time is much less favourable as Mithraism was reaching (or had reached) the decline in its favourability – not least affected by competition with Christianity but also its adoption as the state religion.

By focusing on the locations of Roman establishments (various types of forts, camps etc.) before and around the 212 date and their proximity with symbol stones it should be possible to determine how, when and where the Roman connection was made that caused the "start point" of Pictish-Mithraism.

Where? Roman "establishments" in Pictland – modern day Angus, Aberdeen and Moray – were of variable size from Durno at 141 acres to Strageath at 5 acres. They are difficult to label – hence referring to them as "establishments". They were, from the dictionary definition, places of "residence". At each location, use by the Roman Army could have been of variable duration. Their design, construction, size and location would have been determined by their purpose.

The Roman presence in Pictland was in two geographies separated by "the Mounth" – a range of hills forming an outlying ridge of the Grampians stretching from Ballater in the west to the North Sea coast immediately north of Stonehaven. Their presence was elsewhere in Caledonia but N E Scotland has the concentration of establishments and symbol stones. There are no stones in the vicinity of Hadrian's Wall and few near the Antonine Wall.

The southern of the two geographies had establishments that made up the Gask Ridge and Glen Blockers – shown as yellow squares on the following map.

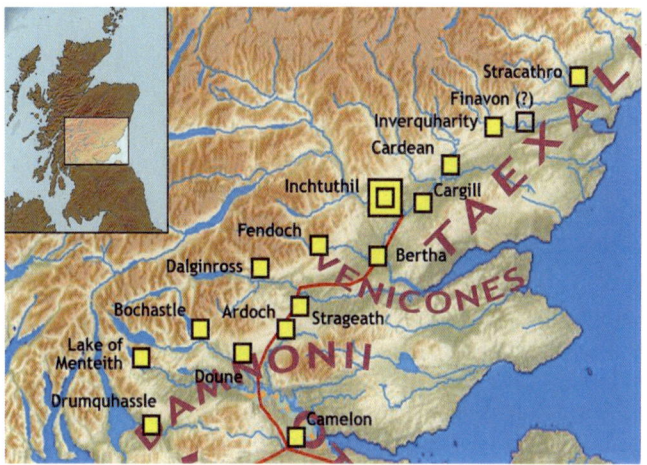

The term "Gask Ridge" can be open to misinterpretation with a notion that it is a natural ridge, is of some considerable length and follows a geographical / geological route (typically referred to as the Highland Line). In fact, it is specifically a 10-mile ridge north of the River Earn in Perthshire. A series of watch / signal-towers was discovered along this ridge terminating at Strageath and Bertha "forts" (see map above).

In trying to set a chronology and grouping for the different Roman establishments in and by Pictland it is useful to take together the so-called Gask Ridge, the so-called Glen Blocker locations plus those establishments so far identified north of the Aberdeen area. It will also be useful to consider that some of these establishments were for the purpose of creating some form of presence so the often-used term "frontier" – a boundary – seems inapplicable.

General Agricola is the common point but his term of office spread over three emperors who together formed the Flavian Dynasty. Preserving the format of naming after emperors, perhaps these establishments could be called the Flavian Invasion Camps.

The size, initial purpose and later re-use of the establishments above is variable.

Here are a few examples:

First established between 80 and 83 during Agricola's campaigns, Camelon, just north of the Antonine wall, is known to have been garrisoned around 86, abandoned around 90 and reoccupied around 139 when the Antonine wall was being built.

Drumquhassle, Doune and Bochastle are Glen Blockers (or Glen Forts) variously from Flavian, Agricolan and Sallustius Lucullus periods – 80 to 86.

Ardoch comprises 6 camps collectively: a large fort with separate sites, annexes and later re-use. Possibly established around 85 by Agricola or his successor, Sallustius Lucullus, and reused at the time of the Antonine Wall construction.

A fort and marching camp at Strageath was built around 80, abandoned around 85 then rebuilt and occupied after the Glen Blockers were abandoned in 86/87.

Agricola's advance HQ for invading Caledonia was built in 82/83 at Inchtuthil but abandoned in 86/87. It was also noted as a Glen Blocker.

Inverquharity is a Flavian period Glen Blocker.

In 79 Agricola invaded southern Scotland advancing to the River Tay. He had the Forth and Clyde forts built, initiated the building of a road network, campaigned in Galloway and Ayrshire in 81, campaigned north of the River Tay in 82 and built Inchtuthil for the XX Legion prior to the battle of Mons Graupius of 83/84. His successor built Glen Blockers up to, maybe beyond, Stracathro and, in turn, his successor (Metilius Nepos) gave up establishments north of the Tay. The combination of Gask Ridge and Glen Blocker camps and forts lasted around ten years until about 90 CE.

Here is North East Scotland, beyond the Mounth, to complete the picture of the Roman presence in Pictland.

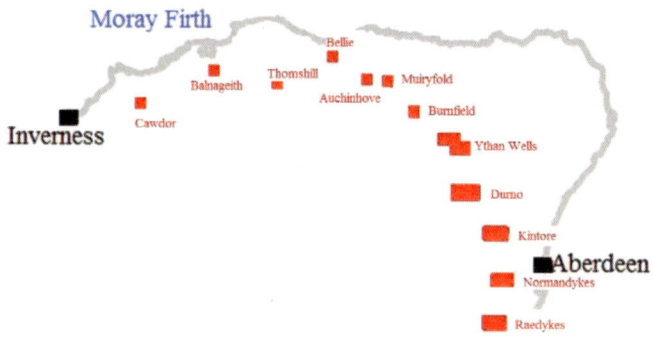

Roman Establishments in North East Scotland ■

These establishments continued beyond Stracathro (the northernmost of the forts shown on the Gask Ridge map) and with similar time periods.

A large establishment (around 100 acres – sufficient to accommodate 16,000 troops) at Raedykes was probably built in the Agricolan period, maybe being reused in Severan times. Less than a day's march north, Normandykes is of similar size.

Two camps at Deer's Den, Kintore date most notably to Septimius Severus and perhaps, also, Agricola. Large scale at over 100 acres the area has revealed Neolithic, Bronze and Iron Age discoveries.

Another large site (of 141 acres) at Durno has Agricolan origins. Immediately to the west is a clear view of Bennachie – a well-known and much supported prime contender for the battle of Mons Graupius.

The larger of the Ythan Wells, Glenmailen camps is considered to be Agricolan.

Burnfield on the south bank of the River Deveron near Rothiemay dates to 83 with the Roman expedition crossing the river on the way to Auchinhove.

Muiryfold, on the South East facing slope of Gallow Hill with a view over the valleys of the Rivers Deveron and Isla was of 109 acres and created by Septimius Severus around 210.

Auchinhove (created in 84 by Argicola and a similar size – about 30 acres – to Ythan Wells Camp 2) is 1½ miles from Muiryfold.

Bellie camp has been eroded by the River Spey.

A site at Easter Galcantray, Cawdor seemingly used only in 84 and 85 is a contender for another Roman fort.

This area does not have the feature of Glen Blocker forts of further south but has significant geographical aspects such as the Mounth on the southern edge of Strathdee and its crossings, Bennachie near Inverurie and narrower rivers which may have determined a different strategy for fort locations.

Timing – a more accurate "when"

Much of the Roman Army activity in these locations was before "the walls" were built. Hadrian's Wall was constructed and actively used between 122 and 138, being placed in a support role then abandoned to 164 when it was re-occupied to 401. The Antonine wall and associated forts were built between 142 and 154 with the outlying forts using the general arrangement of the Gask Ridge installations of the 80s. It was partially "mothballed" between 162 and 165.

In 208 Septimius Severus visited Britannia and initiated repairs to Hadrian's Wall and the Antonine wall.

Septimius Severus campaigned north of the Forth between 208 and 210 building the camp at Carpow. From 211 onwards distractions elsewhere took the Roman spotlight off Scotland. Caracalla succeeded Septimius Severus, settled for peace in 212, suspended the campaign in Caledonia and withdrew to Hadrian's Wall.

Symbol stones near Roman Army establishments from Battledykes to Strageath Locations of Class 1 symbol stones have been added to the previous Gask Ridge and Glen Blockers map. The table below shows three groupings of stones in the vicinity of specific establishments.

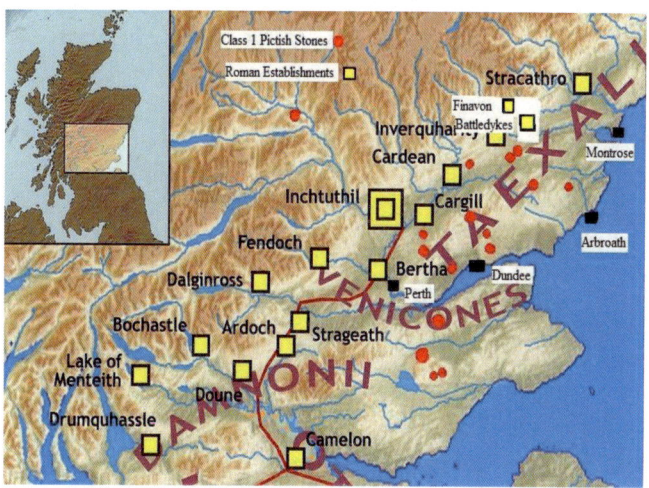

Class 1 stones with legible / discernible symbols are at the following locations in the above area:

Vicinity of:	Class 1 stones at:
Battledykes, Inverquharity & Cardean	Aberlemno, Aberlemno (Flemington), Bruceton, Dunnichen, Kinblethmont
Cargill & Bertha	Cargill, Collace, Keillor, Linlathen, Longforgan, Strathmartine
Strageath	Abdie, Strathmiglo, Westland (Falkland)

In summary, the number of Pictish-Mithraism symbols (as identified in Chapter 6) in the vicinity of: Strageath = 7; Cargill & Bertha = 12; Battledykes, Inverquharity & Cardean = 15.

There is evidence of Severan occupation of Roman Establishments in this geography at Carpow and Battledykes with more of the Agricolan period. This is very relevant to determining when the stones may have been carved with Mithraic symbols – the Agricolan period would have been early for Roman Mithraism (started near the end of the 1st century CE) and the nearest Mithraea were not built nearby until Hadrian's Wall was constructed. There is a low correlation between a Roman presence and the early symbol stones for this geography.

Symbol stones near Roman Army establishments from Muiryfold to Kintore Locations of Class 1 symbol stones have been added to the previous Muiryfold to Kintore map. The table below shows four groupings of stones in the vicinity of specific establishments.

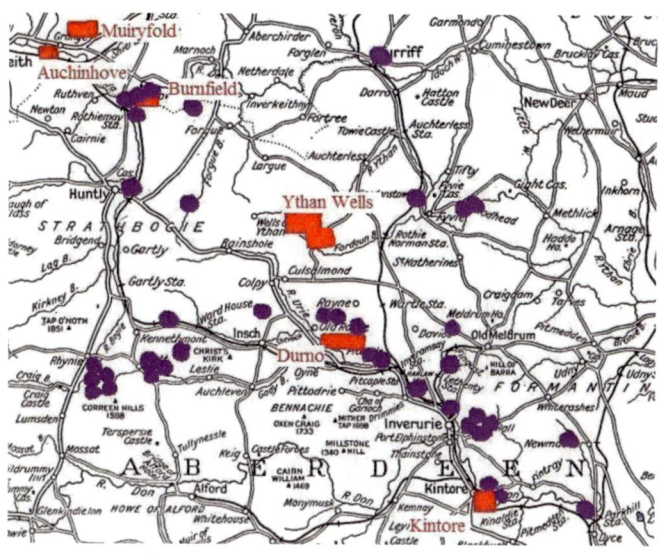

Class 1 stones with legible / discernible symbols are at the following locations in the above area:

Vicinity of:	Class 1 stones at:
Muiryfold, Auchinhove and Burnfield	Huntly & Tillytarmont
Ythan Wells (aka Glenmailen)	Fyvie & Leys of Dummies
Durno	Ardlair (Kennethmont), Bourtie, Brandsbutt, Clatt, Daviot, Drimmies, Logie Elphinstone, Nether Corskie, Newbigging, Newton House, Newton of Lewesk, Picardy, Rhynie & Wantonwells
Kintore	Broomend of Critchie, Cairnton, Dyce, Inverurie, Keith Hall, Kinellar & Kintore (churchyard, Castle Hill & No 4)

In summary the number of Pictish-Mithraism symbols (as identified in Chapter 6) in the vicinity of: Ythan Wells (aka Glenmailen) = 5; Muiryfold, Auchinhove and Burnfield = 13; Kintore = 23; Durno = 46.

In this geography there is a higher concentration of Class 1 stones near to Roman establishments than anywhere else. The large establishments at Muiryfold and Kintore (aka Deer's Den) are from the Severan period. Several others are Agricolan, some having been re-used in Severan times.

With evidence of Severan occupation of Roman establishments in this geography and Mithraea on Hadrian's Wall at the time (plus Mithraea elsewhere in Britannia and on the European mainland) there is a significant correlation between Roman presence and symbol stones. The Severans had a family interest in the pursuit of beliefs, including Roman Mithraism. Septimius Severus's father in law, Julius Bassianus, was high priest for the Temple of the Sun at Emesa (nowadays Homs). His son Caracalla was responsible for the construction of the Baths of Caracalla in Rome which has a Mithraeum underneath. There may well have been other attachments to Mithraism with the military connections of the family. However, on the available evidence no assumption can be made that a Severan Emperor directly influenced the setting up of a form of Mithraism to be practised in Pictland.

Arriving, Going, Staying

Many of the early stones are in the vicinity of known Roman establishments – there may be as yet undiscovered Roman establishments in the vicinity of other early stones e.g. in the Spey valley. From extensive mapping of Roman camps and Pictish Stones, the analysis of the location and incidence of symbols plus the active practice of Roman

Mithraism the conclusion is that it was around the Severan period that symbol stones appeared.

The Roman presence in Pictland around the 212 period was short – about three years. In that time there would have been many troop movements across the areas shown above most likely restricting any settling down except, perhaps, for those operating the larger camps. This gives two options for who might have created Pictish-Mithraism – those who have been "arriving and going" or "staying"?

"Arriving and going" can be seen in the various presences of the Roman military (and no doubt others such as traders and civilian supporters) in Pictland between 79 and 212 (over 130 years). The withdrawal of the army, Caracalla's settling for "peace" with the Caledonians, members of the army being pensioned off at the end of their service and potentially others not required to go to the army's next destination could all result in people "staying". With the Roman army having a proportion of members who were soldiers and auxiliaries from wide areas of the Empire (anywhere other than Rome) perhaps there was reduced resentment by the local population making "staying" a positive option.

At any given time, the military personnel may have thought their presence could be long term as a successful invading force. In that case they could have built Mithraea as had happened elsewhere in Britannia and Europe. But there is no archaeological evidence of Mithraea in Pictland – not discernible in ruins or outlines of establishments or artefacts such as statuary. An alternative in wishing to continue pursuing the Mysteries of Mithras could be the creation of carvings as we now see on the symbol stones but the prevailing environment would not have been conducive – this time was not a time of peace so freedom of movement and activity for military personnel was probably much restricted.

This leads to the source of the carved symbols being people with the intimate knowledge of Roman Mithraism. In other words, the "stayers". As mentioned earlier, if these were people arguably of an ethnicity acceptable (or at least not objectionable) to the local population then there would have been the opportunity for them to practice their religious belief, most likely to extend its reach.

Having concluded that ex-Roman Army "stayers" with Mithraic knowledge remained in Pictland the challenge is to determine a location for the physical "start point" for a symbol stone, or stones, to qualify for being sufficiently feature rich to be used as a place to practise the religious belief.

The First Stone – or Stones

The locations of the Severan Establishments and nearby stones in Pictland are in two broad areas – the Gask Ridge & Glen Blockers and Muiryfold to Kintore. Considering their relative content of establishments and stones, there is a higher correlation between a Roman presence and the early symbol stones in the Muiryfold to Kintore geography. Within that geography 14 of the 27 stones are in the vicinity of Durno with 46 of the 87 symbols.

Just under half of the symbols in the vicinity of Durno are at or near Rhynie – around 10 miles distant. In stone and symbol volume terms the Durno area would appear to be a prime contender for finding the location of the first stone(s) but the largest Severan establishments are at Muiryfold and Kintore (aka Deer's Den).

Maybe a better way of determining which stone or stones could have been the first carved by the "stayers" is by considering the range of symbols, especially those that convey the principles of Roman Mithraism – the greater the range the more that can be explained.

The "top five" symbols for all Class 1 stones are – V-Rod & Crescent, Mirror, Z-Rod & Double Disc, Pictish Beast and Comb.

To narrow down the options, as a first search stone locations with three or more of these symbols are Bourtie, Clatt, Daviot, Logie Elphinstone, Rhynie, Inverurie, Keith Hall, Kintore (Castle Hill), Tillytarmont and Fyvie.

Three of these locations have multiple instances of the selected symbols and additional symbols – Clatt, Rhynie and Tillytarmont. Each of these locations has the range of symbols over more than one stone. The Clatt Stones are fragments – so there may have been further symbols. Rhynie has eight stones currently in a number of locations. Tillytarmont has five stones all found at Donaldson's Haugh at the confluence of the rivers Isla and Deveron.

Symbols on the Tillytarmont Stones:

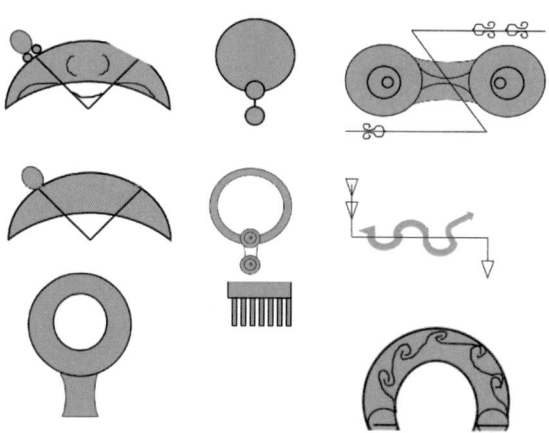

With the broad selection of symbols concentrated in a small space and located between two rivers the case for Tillytarmont having a purpose well beyond that of a stand-alone symbol stone is strong.

When all the stones stood together at the same time there would have been an opportunity to introduce the basics of the Mysteries of Mithras through to more esoteric aspects by progression through the Mithraic grades.

Tillytarmont is put forward as the location of the first stones.

9
CHANGES IN BELIEFS – STONE USAGE, TIMELINES & TRANSITIONS

With the era and original geography of the symbol stones as a pivot point, one can look backwards in time to consider previous religious beliefs but also forwards to identify any prospective influence that Pictish-Mithraism might have had.

Before Pictish-Mithraism:

Some of the symbol stones likely started life as stones within a circle, many have been re-used in building construction, others have lain under churches, a few are most likely in their original locations but none are currently used for their original intent. For a stone carved in 250 CE and still in the same place it will have been seen by around 70 generations; if it was used before in a circle built in the middle/late Bronze Age, then around double that number of generations will have seen the stone. What is amazing is that so many have survived.

Whilst physically the re-used stones have had uses in different religious beliefs there does not appear to be any forward transfer of iconography. This again reinforces the uniqueness and intrigue of the Pictish Symbol Stones.

Over the same period there have been many changes in belief in the geography we are considering. From Stone, Bronze and Iron Ages via so-called pagan, to Christian and many others. Many of the "believers" would recognise the relatively recent, "I to the hills will lift mine eyes".

After Pictish-Mithraism:
In the same manner that Roman Mithraism has not just influenced but arguably has been the predecessor to Pictish-Mithraism, perhaps Pictish-Mithraism has had a similar impact directly or indirectly to successor beliefs. Maybe one of those beliefs is what we know as Freemasonry.

Towards Pictish-Mithraism then Transition to Christianity

A Common Era (CE) time sequence for the physical usage of stones for use with beliefs could be:

```
<-----------Bronze Age ---------------->
                    <----------- Iron Age --------->
 -2000 -1750 -1500 -1250 -1000 -750 -500 -250 0 250

    < Picts >
       < Christianity----------------------->
 0 250 500 750 1000 1250 1500... 2000+
   < P-M >
```

P-M = Pictish-Mithraism

The use and re-use of such stones ranges from the pre-Pictish period (when there would have been an initial use, then in some instances later re-use, of Bronze or Iron Age monoliths or stones in circles), Pictish before Pictish-Mithraism, Pictish-Mithraism and Christian. In the Pictish Mithraic time period some other contemporaneous carvings were included on the stones – for example what appear to be Celtic symbols.

Class 1 slabs had so-called Pictish symbols only. Class 2 had both Pictish and Christian objects (introducing Christianity and, no doubt, used in converting those with, then, current religious beliefs) and Class 3 had Christian symbols only. The general view is a time progression between Classes but Class 1 and 2 could have been created in the same time period, perhaps in different parts of Pictland. Certainly Class 2 stones with Christian and Mithraic iconography are, in effect, transition stones from one religious belief to another. Few locations have both original Pictish Symbol Stones and transition stones (this may simply be due to population movements) but both types of stone are found in, under and around churches.

Considering the broadly 600 to 1000 CE time slot the designs on Cross slabs suggest initially the influence of Celtic or Insular Christianity later replaced by Roman Christianity. During the latter part of this period Viking arrival and settlement could have had an effect on Cross slab design. There is similarity between some objects such as the beast with exaggerated claws and intertwined beasts that are similar to styles used in Norway around 1000 CE – examples can be seen in a Cast Court of the Victoria & Albert museum, London.

An example of a standing stone that has seen a long life is the Craw Stane at Rhynie. Crop marks followed by geophysical investigations surrounding and adjacent to the stone have revealed what would have been Bronze and Iron Age structures.

Class 2 stones have "Christian" crosses. Apart from introducing a different religious belief, the new symbols of Cross, Biblical stories etc. probably would have been used to convert Mithraists. The fact that these stones have symbols from more than one religious belief suggests they were quite acceptable to the remaining Mithraists. Maybe there were distinct transition features in the new iconography such as the arms of the cross being considered to represent the four "elements" of earth, air, fire and water.

Looking to the earlier transition and introduction to Pictish-Mithraism from Roman Mithraism there are no Tauroctonies on standing stones but some components such as the serpent. Several stones engraved with bulls came from Burghead – perhaps a hang back to the Roman Mithraic Tauroctony or maybe that form of Mithraism was practiced there. The well which would have been within the fort boundary could be a Mithraeum. The situation at Burghead may well be one of timing with Roman Mithraism being practised there in the same period as at Hadrian's Wall.

The following pictures show examples of stone circles. The one at Lagmore is near Inveravon church where there are four symbol stones previously attached to an outer wall now in a porch. The church also overlooks the River Spey. Ardlair Stone Circle, like Upper Lagmore has a panoramic view and is near Rhynie and nearby standing stone sites.

Inveravon church has Class 1 stones seemingly from around the 6th to 8th Century, the church itself being erected in 1806 on the site of the previous church built in 1568.

Upper (or West) Lagmore Stone Circle above Ballindalloch Golf Course (near Inveravon Church & Stones) Early Bronze Age.

Class 1 Pictish Standing Stones at Inveravon Church. 6th to 8th Century CE. (Stones now in a porch).

Ardlair Stone Circle (near Kennethmont) – distant view.

And finally two views involving Migvie; the Cairngorms from the graveyard, taken from beside the Migvie Pictish Symbol Stone and an inside view of the current church – restored in 2001 with extensive Christian and Pictish iconography.

Chairs and table inside Migvie church. Restored by Philip Astor of Tillypronie in 2001 in memory of his parents.

The carvings include Pictish symbols (in this picture the V-Rod & Crescent), text in English and at right angles to it in Ogham.

The church has a mixture of Christian and Pictish iconography.

Cairngorms from Migvie grave yard.

A Pictish Cross slab is just beyond the right side of this view.

The beliefs and changes in beliefs in the foregoing and as alluded to in the pictures above cover a period from prospectively 2000 BCE to now – a time span of 4000 years.

Across these changes there seems to have been some form of continued reverence, acceptance or superstition (but no apparent threat).

10
THE OVERALL PICTISH-MITHRAISM® DISCOVERY

Realising the similarity of the shape of the Z-Rod on Pictish Symbol Stones and the shape made by the torches of Cautes and Cautopates on the Mithraic Tauroctony in the Museum of London marked the start of the author's discovery. When investigating Mithraism in more depth it became clear that other symbols might represent aspects of this religious belief – such as the V in the V-Rod being directional arrows so tying in with the travel of the soul on birth and death. By re-evaluating what had been taught at school about the Roman Empire not extending beyond the Antonine Wall led to thinking about who might have created the stones other than the Picts. The result is a breakthrough in decoding the symbols and the discovery of a previously unknown religious belief which the author has called Pictish-Mithraism – now a registered trade mark.

Specifically, the author's research has not only established the link between the iconography contained within the indoor Roman Mithraeum and the symbols on the stones but also who first created them, where and when – altogether constituting the overall Pictish-Mithraism discovery giving answers to, "why so intriguing?"

The key conclusions are:
I The stones had a religious purpose – from the outset
II The "enigmatic" symbols on the stones are Mithraic

III Roman Army "stayers" created the initial symbol stones

I The stones had a religious purpose – from the outset

A process of elimination ruled out some non-religious uses for the stones. Erection as boundary markers was unlikely due to a lack of pattern or layout to their location. Some have considered they could have been commemorative or recorded family lineage, but why adorn them with symbols which require considerable decoding?

The purpose is religious and the context is in two phases – Mithraic and Christian with a distinct overlap between the two.

The second, Christian phase is evidenced by the carving of Christian (or Latin) crosses and images referring to Bible stories. The crosses have an art style that suggests a Northumbrian influence which in turn suggests, at the time, the adoption of the Roman rather than Celtic (or Irish) form of Christianity. This second phase is straightforward to decode with much historical material to assist. The real challenge was the earlier phase.

Despite having seen shapes on a Mithraic Tauroctony that were similar to the Z-Rod symbol, the author still considered contenders such as Manichaeism, a range of Celtic Gods, Persian and Indian versions of early Mithraism, Hinduism, a range of Assyrian Gods and Zoroastrianism. These were all eliminated; for example, there is no aspect in the symbols such as Mazda versus Ahriman in Zoroastrianism. By decoding the symbols that could be seen to represent the theology of the Mithras cult and by relating some symbols to the layouts of temples, evidence for a religion derived from Roman Mithraism built up.

II The "enigmatic" symbols on the stones are Mithraic

Within many religious beliefs there is a great interest in the "afterlife", in immortality and the travel of the soul on death – Mithraism is no exception and this is reflected in the symbols.

The most numerous symbols are the so-called V-Rod & Crescent, Mirror, Z-Rod & Double Disc, Pictish Beast and Comb. Collectively these account for two thirds of the symbols. Several other shapes have been decoded but there is sufficient evidence in these examples to amply demonstrate that the Pictish Symbol Stones were used within the practice of the Mysteries of Mithras.

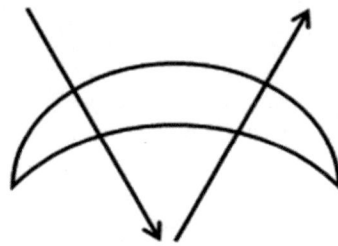

The V-Rod and Crescent, the most numerous of the symbols on the stones, has been decoded as representing the travel of the soul on birth and on death. Rather than a "V", the lines are directional arrows, the angle between them represents the passage of time between the arrival of the soul on birth, into mortality, and its departure on death, into immortality. The Crescent is the skyward view from Earth, across the horizon to the moving planets and the fixed stars of the celestial sphere – beyond is Heaven. The symbolism should, therefore, be spiritually comforting as the returning arrow is suggesting there is not absolute finality on death – this is an enticement to follow Mithraism. The celestial sphere can be considered to represent the Milky Way –

astrologically the home of the soul. Astrologically souls descend on birth through the Gate of Cancer and ascend after death through the Gate of Capricorn. This suggests that the upward arrow passes through the celestial sphere at the Capricorn "gate".

The Mirror circles can be considered to depict relationships between the zodiac, planets and the Earth. Many instances have small connected circles similar to the Double Discs seen with Z-Rods – these represent the Earth, planets and celestial sphere. A larger circle (as alongside) is the zodiac – here more obvious in the "ring" version (rather than the "solid" one) as that is how the zodiac is shown in Mithras group statuary in Roman Mithraea. Where the Double Disc meets or overlaps the zodiac circle this point can be considered to be Capricorn. A link between the V-Rod & Crescent and Mirror symbols involving Capricorn can, therefore, be made – the soul on its return to Heaven. A further decode for the Mirror symbol is the concept of a contract between Mithras and the universe and all it contains – between the invisible and the visible.

Further reinforcing the importance of the Capricorn constellation is the decode for the Pictish Beast. From its shape the Pictish Beast can be seen as the "sea goat" which is the sign of Capricorn. On a symbol stone it could act as a "pointer" to that constellation in the skyward view and enable, with reference to the V-Rod & Crescent, an explanation of the travel of the soul back to Heaven on death. With a fundamental Mithraic belief of the soul enduring in immortality on a person's death the significance of signposting the portal to Heaven (which also features in the Mirror symbol) is reinforced.

These three symbols above share a Capricorn connection important to the Mysteries of Mithras but also with some astrological relationship.

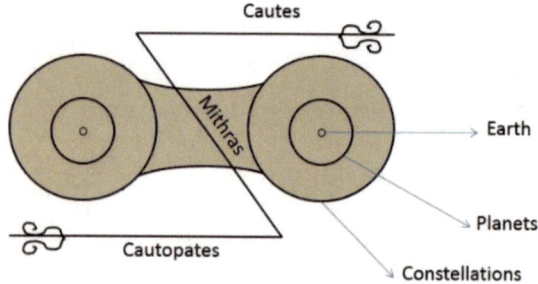

Several aspects of Mithraism are evident in the Z-Rod & Double Disc symbol. In Mithraea Cautes and Cautopates as companions of Mithras indicate, with their torches, life / death, light / darkness and the equinoxes – these are the arms of the "Z" (Mithras being the joining line).

The concentric circles of the Double Discs represent the Earth, the moving planets and the celestial sphere. The "waist" effect of the lines that connect the Discs gives a three-dimensional representation of a dough-ring type shape – this is very significant as it suggests the concept of a "contained" universe.

With the line joining the arms of the "Z" always drawn on stones so that it overlays the connection between the Double Discs we can see that Mithras is external to the contained universe. Being external to it he is also able to rotate the Universe from outside – an aspect brought forward from Persian Mithraism.

Comb symbols can allude to the Mithraic belief of the soul's steps via the planets between the celestial sphere and the Earth at one's birth (into mortality) and back the way to immortality on one's death; particularly relevant when they have 7 "teeth" as there were 7 Mithraic grades and 7 Planets (including, at the time, the Sun and Moon).

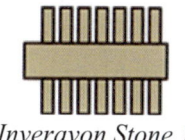

Inveravon Stone 1

III Roman Army "stayers" created the initial symbol stones

With the stones being known for so long as the Pictish Symbol (or Standing) Stones combined with the general view that Pictish (arguably an era and location) is basically interchangeable with Pict, the assumption has been (and still tends to be) that the Picts created the symbol stones. The much greater likelihood is that the existing population did not create or use (initially anyway) the symbol stones –

Roman Army "stayers" did. A previous view of when they could have stayed was when the Army started to withdraw from Britannia around 400 CE but at that time there was no known Roman presence in North East Scotland – the nearest was Hadrian's Wall.

Knowing the imagery inside Roman Mithraea and having knowledge of the planets and constellations of the zodiac in a Mithraic context, believers who became "stayers" were those best placed to make a translation into well coded symbols then place them on suitable material. An astronomical relationship is clear with the Pictish Symbol Stones, as the terrestrial part of the Open Air Mithraeum, being created to enable a complementary interaction by a "believer" between a stone and the skyward view. Several symbols have astronomical links such as the V-Rod & Crescent with the Milky Way, the Triple Disc with the Crater or Cup constellation and Capricorn plus other associations between animal, mythological and human objects with Zodiacal items. The interpretations of Cautes looking to the East and Cautopates to the west, the use of the morning and evening star, identification of and with the equinoxes point to a combination of the use of astronomy with geography.

Establishing the "start" for Pictish-Mithraism – where, when and by whom – progressively pointed towards a location in Pictland where there had been a Roman Army presence with structured withdrawal. Two broad areas on either side of the Mounth had Roman Army establishments in several timeslots. Periods before the popularity of Roman Mithraism and after the ascendancy of Christianity can be eliminated, leaving the Severan period of 208 to 212 CE.

It was not untypical for a retiring member of the Roman Army to be pensioned off and given the opportunity to stay where he was based; on a withdrawal perhaps that opportunity was extended to more than pensionable members. There was a known end to a Roman presence in North East Scotland around 212 CE under Emperor Caracalla (who created his extensive baths complex in Rome with a Mithraeum underneath). He suspended the Severan campaign in Scotland, withdrew to Hadrian's Wall, and "settled for peace"; the army also moved on to activities outside Britannia. Following the Mysteries of Mithras was popular at this time, especially by army personnel – and encouraged by emperors. It is reasonable to deduce that the "stayers" would have wished to follow their religious belief.

With the broad mix of people from many countries in the Roman Army there is no suggestion that those who stayed were in fact Roman or even from Italy. Perhaps there was either an affinity with the existing population or an acceptance by them of the incoming "stayers" – maybe they were of similar origin. With the mix in the Roman Army of people from different countries, there could have been members from Gaul and Germany (highly likely given the presence there and locations in Gaul sometimes being headquarters for those who governed Britain) or from countries further east where there was knowledge of other forms of Mithraism. Whichever might be a source prospect, as members of the Roman Army they would have been familiar with the cult and its practices, which had a central following in and around Rome as can be seen from the existing remains of Mithraea and in many of the acquired provinces. All roads lead to and from Rome – including Mithraic ones!

Placing the Roman Army establishments north and south of the Mounth onto a map, followed by adding in Class 1 stone locations, indicated proximity between stone sites prompting, in the analysis, elimination of pre-Severan establishments.

Based on "stayers" practicing Mithraism, prospectively expanding its following, a wide range of symbols in a small geographic area was sought – together with proximity to a Severan establishment. In the analysis Muiryfold and Kintore areas were prime contenders – large establishments both from the Severan period. Muiryfold has been described as having good views along the valleys of the Rivers Isla and Deveron.

The widest range of symbols in the author's analyses is at the cluster of stones at Tillytarmont by the confluence of the Rivers Isla and Deveron. Tillytarmont is put forward as the geographic start point for that successor to Roman Mithraism – Pictish-Mithraism.

A Roman Legacy

Because of the enduring intrigue of what they represented and who created them, arguably the symbols on the stones are the biggest legacy the Romans left in Britain.

APPENDIX 1
PICTISH SYMBOL STONES
CASE STUDIES

Two case studies are shown in Chapter 7 – "Stones & Distant Views". This further selection is also from either side of the Mounth – a range of hills forming an outlying ridge of the Grampians from Ballater to the North Sea coast – and includes both Class1 and Class 2 stones.

Individual and groups of objects on Pictish Symbol Stones serve to enable a message to be put over albeit often obscured in keeping with the Mysteries of Mithras (for Class 1 stones) or a story from the Christian bible (for Class 2 stones). Additionally, there are elements of transition between religious beliefs. These seem to be low key from Celtic pagan to Pictish-Mithraism and high profile from Mithraism to Christianity – a prime purpose of Class 2 with mixed iconography is this transition. Class 3 stones with Christian symbolism only are not included.

Photographs, sketches and drawings in this Appendix are © Norman J Penny.

Locations by RCAHMS Site Number for all objects on the symbol stones are in Appendix F at www.pictish-mithraism.com.

Site Name	General Location	RCAHMS Site Number
Bruceton	Blairgowrie	NO25SE 17
Cossans	Forfar	NO45SW 4
Dunfallandy	Pitlochry	NN95NW 29
Inveravon	Aberlour / Grantown	NJ13NE 7
Kintore	Inverurie	NJ17NE 32 & 33; NJ71NE 69
Maiden Stone	Inverurie	NJ72SW 1
Rhynie	Huntly	NJ42NE 22, 30, 35, 36, 52 & 53
Tullich	Ballater	NO39NE 2

Bruceton

Features – this simply incised Class 1 stone is near a river in a sloping open ground location and has two of the more commonplace symbol designs.

There are other standing stones in the vicinity, seemingly without carvings, so this one could be part of a set of stones with some other significance (maybe pre-Pictish period). Human bones have been discovered nearby and cists found in the mid-1800s within 18m of the stone. This area either side of the current Perth / Angus boundary has a concentrated collection of stone sites, the nearest to Bruceton being predominantly Class 2. However, north east and less than 20 miles away is Aberlemno Flemington Farm and a stone with the same two carvings.

With a right angle in its course, the view from the stone is down to and across the River Isla in the south and east. Water appears to be of significance in Pictish-Mithraism with over 15% of locations identified as adjacent to rivers and burns.

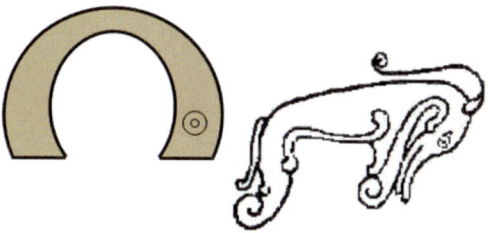

The symbols popularly referred to as the Horseshoe / Arch and Pictish Beast are the only two visible on this stone – the Arch uppermost. The Horseshoe is plain except for two concentric circles in the lower right.

The Arch is the view into the Roman Mithraeum with its tunnel type shape and the Arch is also the shape at the so-called Tauroctony end which would have housed the Tauroctony statue. It could also represent the skyward view to the zodiac.

The Pictish Beast is decoded as the "sea goat" which is Capricorn – astrologically the Gate of the Gods through which the soul travels on death into immortality. In Pictish-Mithraism, the connection between the V-Rod & Crescent, the Mirror and the Pictish Beast symbols is Capricorn. On a symbol stone the Pictish beast could act as a "pointer" to the Capricorn constellation and, with Reference to the V-Rod & Crescent, enable an explanation of the soul's travel via the celestial sphere back to Heaven, and immortality, on death.

Being Class 1 and of a simple design, these two symbols at Bruceton, nearby at Aberlemno Flemington Farm and also at Congash in Badenoch and Strathspey could be a reminder of Roman Mithraism to people locating to these areas.

Cossans, St Orlands Stone

Features – with a mixture of commonplace and rarer designs including a "one-off" this Class 2 stone is in an isolated, open location and overlooks water. On some maps it is shown as Cossins.

An isolated position in low lying fields (prospectively an original location), six inhumations found in the mid-1800s with 5 in cists and the "one-off" carving of six figures in a boat are a few aspects that make this stone noteworthy.

Furthermore, deep recesses around the ringed Celtic Cross have Interlaced Animals on each side of the vertical. On the left a pair biting beak to beak, another pair biting beak to tail, one higher up alone and on the right several which are not readily decipherable.

This imagery is taken to the reverse of the stone where two creatures with heads opposing at the top of the stone have opposing fish style tails at the bottom connected by interlaced patterns on the sides of the stone – they appear to be fighting over what presumably is food. None of these objects suggests any specific story or message.

Register type layout is used on the reverse from a V-Rod & Crescent then Z-Rod and Double Disc at the top then an area that has been removed, a hunting scene in two registers – the top having two riders and the lower another two riders followed by two dogs, the figures in a boat and, finally, a Beast with Exaggerated Claws facing (attacking?) a cow. Decoding the objects is difficult except for the V-Rod & Crescent and Z-Rod & Double Disc (see the case study for Aberlemno for an outline explanation).

The name of the stone gives no clues either as St Orland is not on any "saint lists", or similar, researched so far; perhaps it is a corruption of another name. However, its location and proximity to the Dean Water (due south) and Loch of Forfar (due north east) plus all its symbols and imagery reinforced by the likely spirituality of the adjacent burials makes this is a prime example of a transition stone (between Pictish-Mithraism and Christian beliefs).

Dunfallandy

Features – symbol rich with people, animals, fantastic beasts etc. this Class 2 so-called "Priest's Stone" [Clach an T'Sagart in Gaelic] is near a river and the site of an old chapel. Notably a scene alludes to a biblical story.

Reputedly located near Dunfallandy chapel (no ruins remain) and near to a private grave yard it is possible that this stone is more or less in its original position. It is very close to the River Tummel (just to the east) with some similar design styles to the symbol stone no more than 5 miles away at Logierait (the Double Disc and Hippocamp type beasts in particular).

Another example of a transition stone (from Mithraic to Christian) but with the Class 1 elements low key, certainly in size, with two Pictish Beasts (Capricorn shapes) plus two examples of the V-Rod & Crescent and one of the Z-Rod & Double Disc (see the case study for Aberlemno for an explanation). Abernethy has the only other example of the hammer and anvil objects and Rosskeen the only other tongs – their significance in terms of a religious belief are elusive, maybe they just represent the carver's other skills (not restricted to stone carving). Hammer and tongs also allude to Vulcan with linkages to fire – one of the four classical elements.

Like Cossans, there are two creatures with heads opposing at the top of the reverse of the stone connecting to fish style tails at the bottom– they appear to be pulling on either side of an animal with long ears (the eyes and nose like a dog are apparent).

The Cross side has five Beasts with Exaggerated Claws, two interlaced animals (facing one another horizontally head to head) and another beast (a fish monster which looks like a form of Hippocamp) initially seems to have human legs protruding from its mouth. However, on closer inspection the beast appears to be biting or throwing up the person – maybe alluding to the biblical Jonah coming out of the mouth of the whale (or fish).

Only one other similar object exists, at Woodwrae where human legs are clearly protruding from the beast's mouth. Also, as at Woodwrae, one of the beasts has something in its mouth but here it looks less like prey and more like a stick. Other animals on this stone are a stag and a horse (with rider) which are unconnected – one on the Cross side, the other the reverse.

Apart from the Cross with Bosses on its arms, the other clearly Christian objects are the angels alongside the lower arm of the Cross and on the reverse two people facing one another with a Cross between them – they are said to represent Saints Paul and Anthony who were contemporary and each has been stated as the founder of the monastic way of life. If indeed one of these seated figures is Saint Anthony maybe there is a tie in with some of the objects on the Cross side of the stone which might portray the temptations of the saint together with the story of Anthony seeing angels ascending with the soul of Paul when he died. It has been suggested there is a figure of Jonah on the Cross side – this would fit in with the above mentioned fish monster throwing up a person.

Inveravon

Features – four Class 1 stones, generally with more commonplace symbols, displayed on the wall of a church by the River Spey – recently relocated to the porch. The stone found under the foundation of an old church has a "one- off" design.

V-Rod & Crescent objects appear at the top of twenty Class 1 stones – arguably placed there deliberately so the viewer looks up from the stone to the sky (for smaller stones) or across the top to the sky (for taller stones). The object has been decoded as the crescent representing the celestial sphere and the V-Rod being two directional arrows.

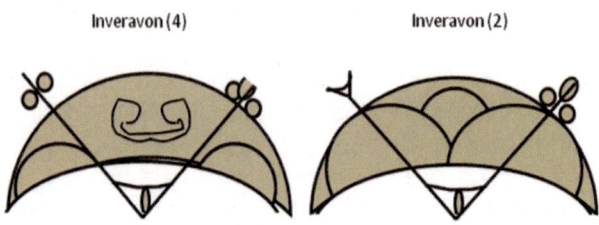

Inveravon (4)   Inveravon (2)

In Pictish-Mithraism the soul comes into mortality from Heaven at birth and returns to immortality at death. These two examples very clearly show the direction of travel (in from the left hand side and out from the right) to a central point (the viewer). Although the two examples at Inveravon have different infill to the crescents, the design at the focal point is the same on both.

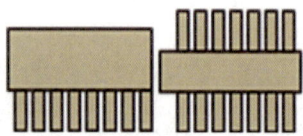

Two stones here have Combs of different designs. On the webpage "Mithraic Symbols – Identified and Decoded" at www.pictish-mithraism.com , twenty-one distinct "comb" designs emerged and have been analysed into four groups. The Inveravon Combs are in separate groups – one has 7 teeth on each side of a central bar, the other has eight teeth below a single bar. The latter is very difficult to see on the stone and, therefore, to decipher – it may have 7 teeth depending on how lines are counted.

The number 7 is of particular importance in Roman Mithraism being the number of planets known in the period – as "gates" it is via these planets that the soul travels from and to the celestial sphere. Also there are 7 Mithraic grades. The presence of features associated with the number 7 on Pictish Symbol Stones further tends to support a follow through from Roman to Pictish-Mithraism.

Combs are never seen without associated Mirrors which fall into two patterns – described elsewhere in this publication as "ring" and "solid".

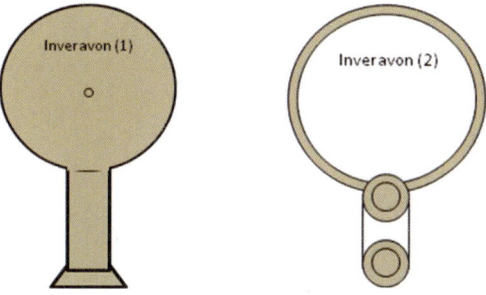

At Inveravon there is one of each, the solid example being on the stone with the Eagle and the Comb with the double row of teeth. This association of Mirrors and Combs could simplify their interpretation. If the Combs have a numeric association with elements of the Mysteries of Mithras (as noted above) and Combs are all seen with Mirrors then, arguably, the Mirror object is also related to the Mysteries. For Inveravon Stone No. 2 the symbol can be decoded as a Double Disc (usually representing the Earth, planets and celestial sphere – but, here, lacking the central dot to depict the Earth) connecting to the zodiac specifically at the constellation Capricorn. Inveravon Stone No. 1 has a one- off for a Mirror design (which does look like a hand-held mirror) but is more like a Mirror Case suggesting some artistic licence or a dual representation including the relationship between Mithras and the zodiac (as with a Mirror Case).

Generally, the Triple Disc looks like a receptacle with carrying rings and has been referred to as a cauldron. Having what looks like a bar or rod across the Triple Disc object at Inveravon brings together two ways of alluding to water as a circle with a horizontal line which is a pagan symbol for water plus the cauldron. Conversely, or additionally, the decode for this symbol has the main circle as the zodiac with the smaller circles as the Cancer and Capricorn constellations – the gates from and to Heaven.

There is a complete Pictish Beast on Stone No. 4 and a fragment, mainly of the head, on Stone No. 3. In addition to the decode being the sea goat as the sign of Capricorn a prospective further meaning is the Leontocephalous (a complex imagery of never ending time). Placed adjacent to the V-Rod and Crescent there is an opportunity for someone to talk through immortality (Capricorn being the gate to Heaven on death) and infinite time together.

On the middle stone on the church wall is an Eagle which in Celtic mythology was seen as one of the oldest creatures whose wisdom and age were only surpassed by the Salmon. Many Pictish Symbol Stones have objects that have Celtic connections.

Certainly the most striking of the objects on the set of Inveravon Stones is the Mirror Case. Like Mirrors, the Mirror Cases have "solid" and "hollow" or ring patterns making classification difficult as a few "solid" examples have a clear outer ring. Whilst the example on Inveravon Stone No. 1 is in the "solid" majority it is a "one-off" due to its arrangement of partial circle plus dots.

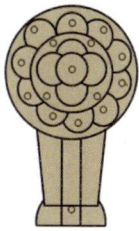

Whereas "hollow" Mirror Cases can fairly readily be explained as representing the birth of Mithras (the lower part of the design being the birth from the rock) and also his holding the zodiac (i.e. the circle ore ring shape) the "solid" objects gave the carver the opportunity to make use of the full space enclosed by the outer circle. In this instance there are three distinct rings (the Earth, the planets and the celestial sphere perhaps); between the outer and first ring in are ten partial circles of slightly differing size with a dot in each; between the first ring in and second are four partial circles with dots in the spaces in between; there is a single dot in the middle. Neither the shapes nor dots nor the numbers of them suggests anything to do with Pictish-Mithraism – maybe like the lines and dots on the Eagle they are merely decorative.

Kintore

Features – several Class 1 stones with typical symbols over two sites (one now a levelled hill) near a river. One of the few examples of connections with the number 7.

Found in three locations – dug up in a church yard, found when Castle Hill was removed for the creation of a railway line and in a garden – these four stones are now in three locations but may at one time have all been together. The raised land could well have had significance when the stones had their original use in the Mysteries of Mithras especially as the location is adjacent to a river – the River Don. Decodes for the Z-Rod and Double Disc, Mirror, Triple Disc with bar and Pictish Beast (there are three at Kintore) are described in case studies above. The Salmon may have Celtic connections symbolising knowledge and wisdom, perhaps reinforced by the stone being next to a river. The rather indistinct Tuning Fork object at Kintore is stylistically different from the other ten examples.

There are three unusual symbols here. Double Crescents of a "back-to-back" configuration are also at Newton of Lewesk, Ulbster and Dunrobin Dairy Park only – drawn by mirror imaging maybe these are more artistic licence than putting over a particular message. There is one other example of a "Concentric" Square at Newton of Lewesk – it is very plain, unlike Kintore where the design has opposed, scallop-like, ornate corners.

Of particular note is the V-Rod and Crescent (picture of stone above and detail drawn below). Although following the "standard" shape the infill here makes this example very much a "one- off". Generically this symbol is decoded as the soul's travel from and to Heaven beyond the celestial sphere. These journeys are via the 7 planets – one of the reasons when the number 7 is of supreme interest in Roman Mithraism. The "dots" on this stone do not appear well on the adjacent photograph so the drawn version is shown above.

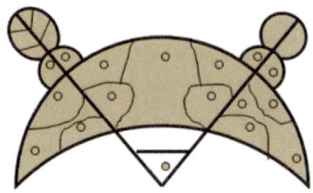

Looking at the clusters of dots, there are 7 dots near the left hand (downward) pointer or arrow – two on the outer of the crescent and five within the crescent. By the right hand (upward) pointer there are eight dots, the "extra" one being just below the pointer compared with the downward pointer

– error or of significance or merely the difficulty in counting the dots when there are other marks on the stone? Between the pointers there are also 7 dots – two on the outer side of the crescent and five within the crescent. It must be remembered that the number of known planets when these carvings were made is not the number known now. The Moon and Sun were also considered to be planets with the Earth at the centre of the planet circles and, indeed, the Universe – not as a planet itself.

Maiden Stone (aka Drumdurno Stone)

Features – possibly standing only a few yards from its original location, this stone has a mix of Mithraic and Christian era carvings.

Often referred to in standing stone books as monsters or fish monsters the objects above the Cross look like Hippocamps except that correctly drawn Hippocamps have horse heads. Several of these objects on Pictish Symbol Stones are difficult to decode due to design variations. Skinnet Chapel at Halkirk and Ulbster creatures have the curled tail, no fore legs and soft features to the head. Meigle No. 1 has four carvings counted in this publication as Hippocamps – three are of the type with a fish like tail, one has a curled tail, the two that are shown opposing both have fish type tails, horse heads and fore legs as does one other object but the example with curled tail has the same soft features in the head design as Halkirk and Ulbster and no forelegs. Brodie and Logierait Stones are similar to the Maiden Stone with opposing, menacing looking creatures with curled tails and no forelegs. Rather confusing but categorised here as Hippocamps in the absence of any alternative classifications. In this instance there is probably a Christian story attached to the Hippocamps with the man standing in between.

Although the top of the stone is weather worn it looks as if the uppermost figures are centaurs as is the figure full-width lower down. Allegories could explain the use of these symbols ranging from the explanation of a Christian story – St Anthony's encounter with a centaur – to more Mithraic interpretations involving the constellation Centaurus, a bull slayer etymology or a pun on bull.

Mirror, Comb and Pictish Beast decodes are outlined in case studies above.

Turning to the Z-Rod with Notched Rectangle, here is an unusual object. Eleven "notched rectangle" objects have been found so far, nine of which are with Z-Rods. Six not only have the notch at the bottom of the rectangle but cut-outs on the left and right verticals. The Z-Rod can be interpreted as those with Double Discs i.e. the torches, albeit rotated ninety degrees, of Cautes and Cautopates representing, respectively, the morning and spring equinox and the evening and autumn equinox.

The Notched Rectangle represents the Roman Mithraeum with side benches and end wall which typically housed the Tauroctony. The side cut-outs represent what are referred to as the cult niches and in an underground Mithraeum would have accommodated statues of Cautes and Cautopates. So this composite object is a reminder of the Roman Mithraeum and could have been used instructionally.

Rhynie

Features – eight stones discovered with church, saint, river and open space associations. Two were discovered in the foundations of an older church another is most likely in its original open location, the remainder found in what is now the village and ploughed up in farmland. One lost and seven currently viewable in three locations. Collectively maybe a contender for "cathedral" type classification.

The "Craw Stane" was apparently given this name as the Pictish Symbol Stone is the only place for a long distance that a crow could sit on and have a wide view. Hence the set of photographs to illustrate the point which equally would apply to a number of people congregating looking outward and to an inward, focal point view from miles around – aspects probably of significance in Pictish-Mithraism. Given the vantage point, the stone seems under-utilised in the way of adornment of carvings but maybe the simplicity is specific with the Salmon having Celtic meaning for knowledge and wisdom and the Pictish Beast with its Capricorn decode may have acted as a pointer to that constellation.

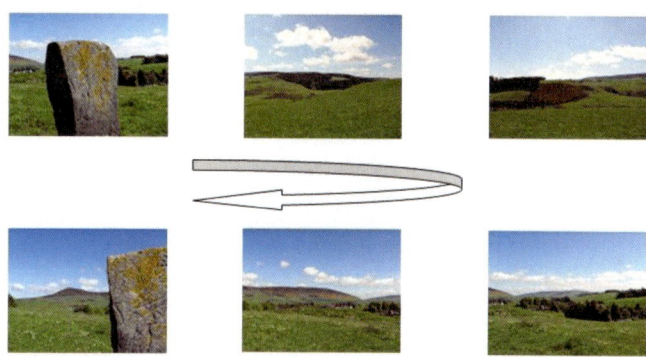

In the left hand side lower photograph the Hill of Noth rises to a peak – the Tap o' Noth – where there is the remains of a vitrified fort and very wide views across what is now Aberdeenshire including the Craw Stane and other forts.

Crop marks followed by geophysical investigations surrounding and adjacent to the Craw Stane have revealed what would have been Bronze and Iron Age structures. With the Iron Age finishing in more remote parts by the end of the Roman period this stone could have been erected at the time of a Roman withdrawal bridging a prospective move from so-called pagan beliefs (using the Salmon) to those of Pictish-Mithraism (using the Pictish Beast representing Capricorn).

Now badly worn, the stones placed on either side of the gate at the north end of Rhynie village square were found in an area that is now the south end of the village.

One has a Z-Rod & Double Disc – a fundamental symbol used to explain the Mysteries of Mithras – the carving on the other stone is of a man carrying a square shield and spear. Also within the area occupied by the village there was a stone recorded over two hundred years ago as having a Pictish Beast, V-Rod & Crescent and what looked like a Mirror Case.

At Barflat Farm next to the old kirkyard, two stones were ploughed up in the late 1970s. The partial stone has a Pictish Beast and what has been assumed to be a Comb but in style is more like a simple Decorated Rectangle with other indecipherable lines. Only three Pictish Symbol Stones show axe-wielding figures – two are engaged in what looks like a fight on the Glamis Manse Stone on the Cross side of what was most likely a reused Class 1 stone i.e. "upgraded" to Class 2; a striding figure holding an axe in front is at Golspie and the example at Rhynie is incised on a large stone which has been relocated to Aberdeenshire Council offices. Their significance is difficult to assess.

Rhynie Old Church is by the Water of Bogie – two stones were discovered in the foundations during the church's demolition. Unlike several other locations where symbol stones have been found when demolishing an old church to replace it with a modern building (typically Victorian era), this one was demolished and its replacement built in the nearby village of Rhynie. The kirk yard continues as a burial place. Originally known as St Luag's church it is difficult to ascertain whether that church was dedicated to the saint or founded by him. St Luag, a contemporary of St Columba, has several other names including St Moluag (the "mo" prefix being an endearment simply for "my dear").

He came from Ireland to Scotland in 562, establishing a community at Lismore then at Rosemarkie and Mortlach – these later became the Roman Sees of the Isles, Ross and Aberdeen. In his time he seemingly founded one hundred churches in what we now call Scotland.

At other locations associated with St Luag (St Moluag) and with potentially contemporaneous symbol stones one, Alyth, is a simple stone with a Cross but Clatt has Class 1 symbols only. So no pointers to suggest St Luag had actually established a church at Rhynie – not least as the stones in the vicinity are all Class 1 and one might expect some Christian iconography at a Mithraic to Christian transition location.

As well as a broad array of typical Pictish Symbol Stone objects on the Rhynie Church Stones, there is a "one-off" which variously has been described as a dog, otter and seal. It is listed in this publication as a "Beast's Head" in the absence of no absolute clarity in the carving. When this stone was moved to its current location thirteen shallow cup marks were discovered. These only appear on Class 1 stones except in the case of Meigle No. 1, a Class 2 stone that is a re-used pre-Pictish era standing stone.

With a location having wide open views (from it and to it), line of sight to/from a hill top fort, an adjacent river, a number of symbol stones with the general array of objects used in Pictish-Mithraism (V-Rod & Crescent, Z-Rod & Double Disc, Mirror, Comb and Pictish Beast), at least one Celtic religious belief object (the Salmon on the Craw Stane) plus identifiable Bronze and Iron Age structures Rhynie could be a contender for what the author has called a "cathedral" site. In other words, it has an importance greater than that of a single stone site that may also not have the prehistorical attachments and topography of Rhynie.

Furthermore, this is arguably a specifically Class 1 "cathedral" location – there are no known transition stones i.e. Class 2 so there may have been a time gap between the end of the Pictish-Mithraism era and the establishment of a Christian Church. Not untypically the original church is located at or nearby a Pictish Mithraist site and named after a Celtic saint. A continuum of religious beliefs can be argued for Rhynie from those of the Bronze and Iron Age people, to Celtic "pagan", Pictish-Mithraism, Celtic Christianity, and Roman Christianity to Church of Scotland.

Tullich

Features – one Class 1 stone is housed by the doorway to the current church with fifteen Cross stones (specifically Class 3). Several church sites have dedications to saints. However, Tullich is rare as its saint, Nathalan (seemingly a native of Deeside), is very likely to have been the founder of the original church here.

Located a few hundred yards from the River Dee, a Celtic chapel was established by St Nathalan (Nachalan or Nachlan or Neachtan) who became the Bishop of Tullich and died in 678. Having been found in the old church, it is assumed that the Pictish Symbol Stone is more or less in its original location. The church has been held by the Knights Templar then the Hospitallers who built a fort round the church in thirteenth century. An interesting "mysteries" theme links from the time of Pictish-Mithraism to the Knights Templar around the twelfth century to the present day – a currently active Freemasons' Lodge chartered in 1815 is named the Lodge of St Nathalan of Tullich-in-Mar.

Considering the stone would most likely have been alone in an open landscape with a surrounding backdrop of hills and mountains (including Lochnagar at over 1,000 metres height in the south west) it is not difficult to imagine someone looking up to the top of the stone to the Z-Rod & Double Disc then to the sky and heavens beyond.

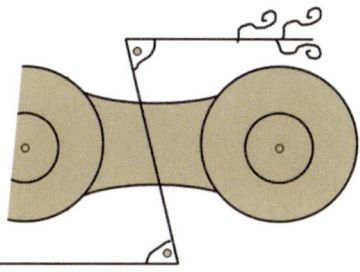

Very similar to Eassie, Dyce (1), Clatt, Keith Hall, Kintore Castle Hill (1), Logie Elphinstone (2), Picardy, Aberlemno Roadside (1) and Cossans. Some of the "flame" carving is missing on the upper rod (the torch held by Cautes signifying morning and the spring equinox) but it reasonably can be assumed there would have been flame carving on the lower rod (Cautopates' torch signifying evening and the autumn equinox).

As usual for this symbol set, the connecting rod alludes to Mithras connecting together the day, the months between equinoxes and time itself. In the discs the central dot is Earth, the inner ring the planets and the outer ring the celestial sphere.

In the middle of this stone is the unmistakeable Pictish Beast with the "lappet" and dolphin-like snout still visible. Style-wise this example is quite unexceptional being one of the two thirds that face to the right and following the standard pattern.

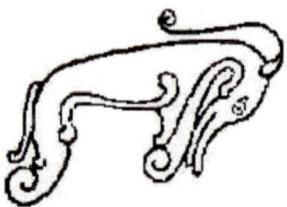

The rationale concluding this is a sea-goat – Capricorn – is on the webpage "Mithraic Symbols – Identified and Decoded" at www.pictish-mithraism.com .

As mentioned before, the Mirror is not a mirror but a symbol within the Mysteries of Mithras so, typically, has been obscured so requires to be decoded. Two general patterns have emerged which refer to the carving style – "ring" and "solid". There is some commonality amongst examples but unlike the Pictish Beast, no standard. Of the style at Tullich there are six other examples at Clatt, Daviot, Keith Hall, Glamis Manse, Aberlemno and Park House which comprise the Double Disc part of the Z-Rod & Double Disc design with the larger circle being the zodiac.

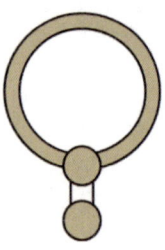

APPENDIX 2
EXAMPLES OF SYMBOL DESIGNS

Pictish Symbol Stones – "V-rod & Crescent" Designs – Examples

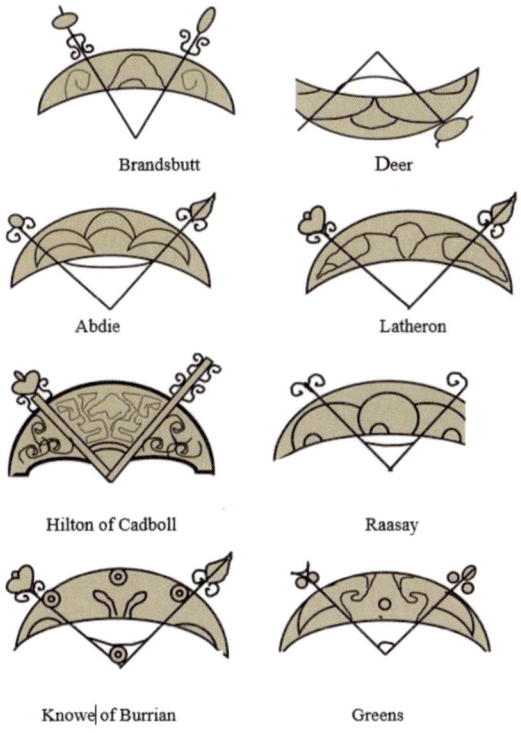

Pictish Symbol Stones – "Mirror" Designs – Examples

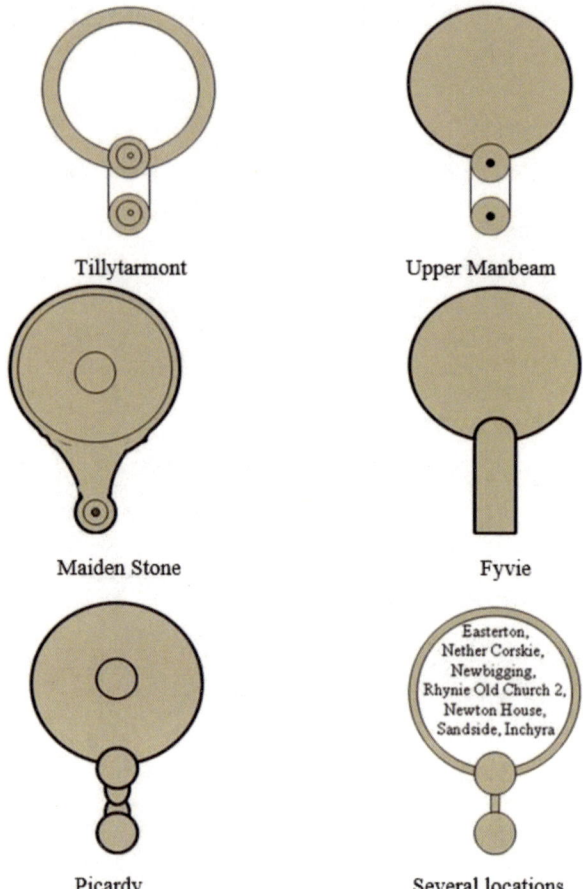

Tillytarmont

Upper Manbeam

Maiden Stone

Fyvie

Picardy

Several locations

Pictish Symbol Stones – "Z-rod & Double Disc" Designs – Examples

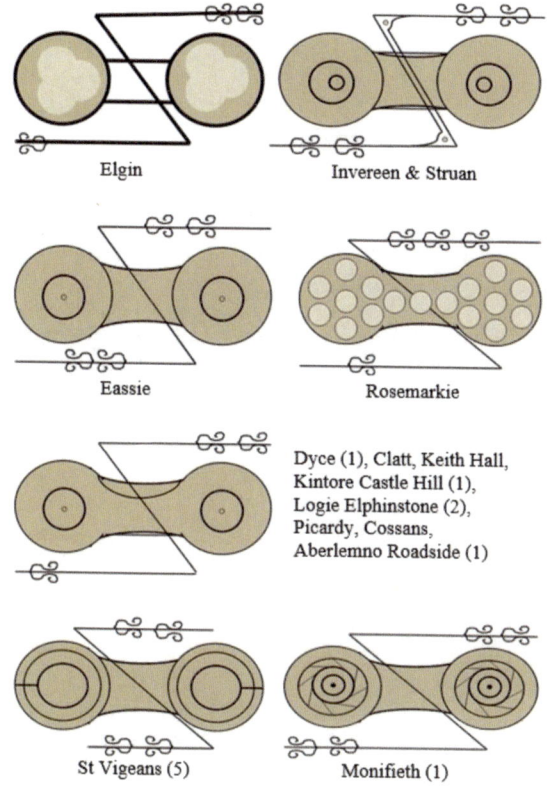

Elgin

Invereen & Struan

Eassie

Rosemarkie

Dyce (1), Clatt, Keith Hall, Kintore Castle Hill (1), Logie Elphinstone (2), Picardy, Cossans, Aberlemno Roadside (1)

St Vigeans (5)

Monifieth (1)

Pictish Symbol Stones – "Comb" Designs – Examples (by group)

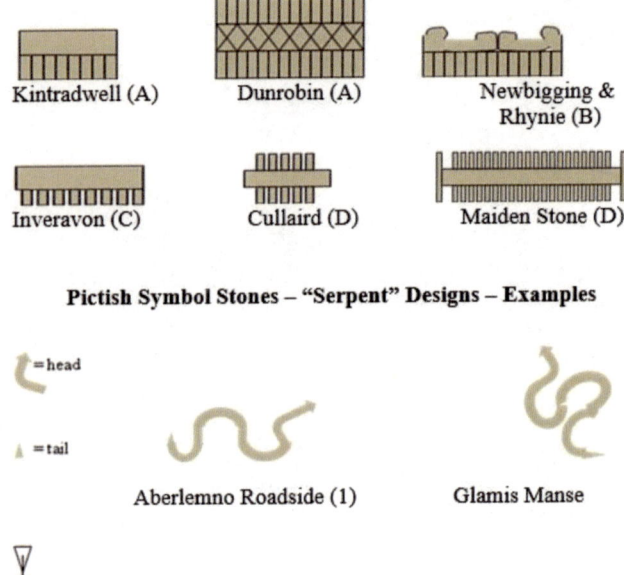

Kintradwell (A) Dunrobin (A) Newbigging & Rhynie (B)

Inveravon (C) Cullaird (D) Maiden Stone (D)

Pictish Symbol Stones – "Serpent" Designs – Examples

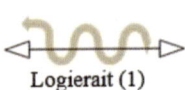
= head

= tail

Aberlemno Roadside (1) Glamis Manse

Tillytarmont Picardy, Balluderon & Drumbuie

Logierait (1) Golspie

Pictish Symbol Stones – "Mirror Case" Designs – Examples

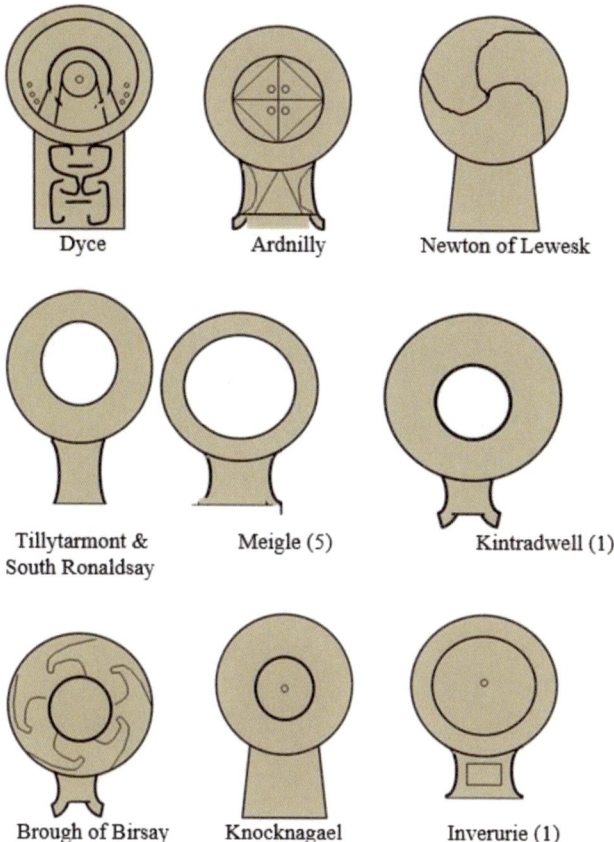

Pictish Symbol Stones – "Double Disc" Designs – Examples

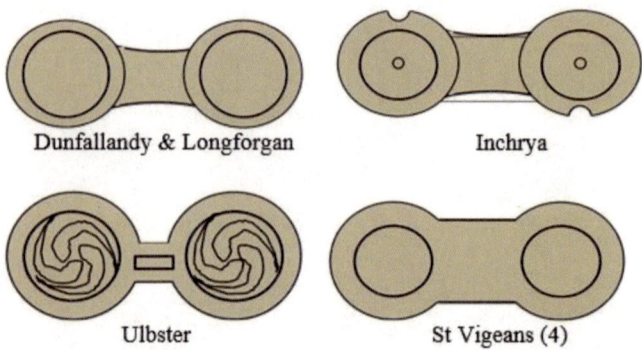

Pictish Symbol Stones – "Horseshoe / Arch" Designs – Examples

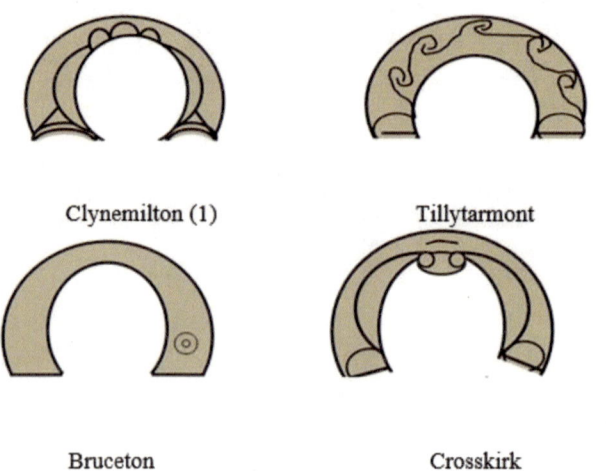

Pictish Symbol Stones – "Decorated Rectangle" Designs – Examples

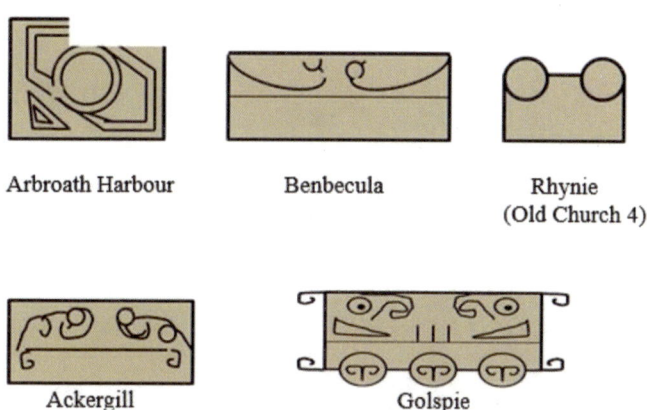

Arbroath Harbour

Benbecula

Rhynie
(Old Church 4)

Ackergill

Golspie

Pictish Symbol Stones – "Tuning Fork" Designs – Examples

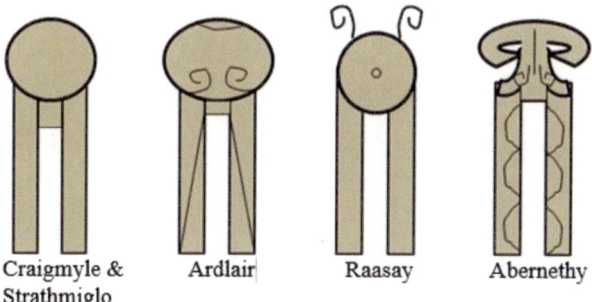

Craigmyle & Strathmiglo

Ardlair

Raasay

Abernethy

Pictish Symbol Stones – "Triple Disc" Designs – Examples

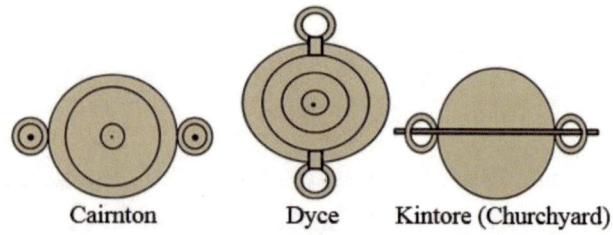

Pictish Symbol Stones – "Notched Rectangle" Designs – Examples

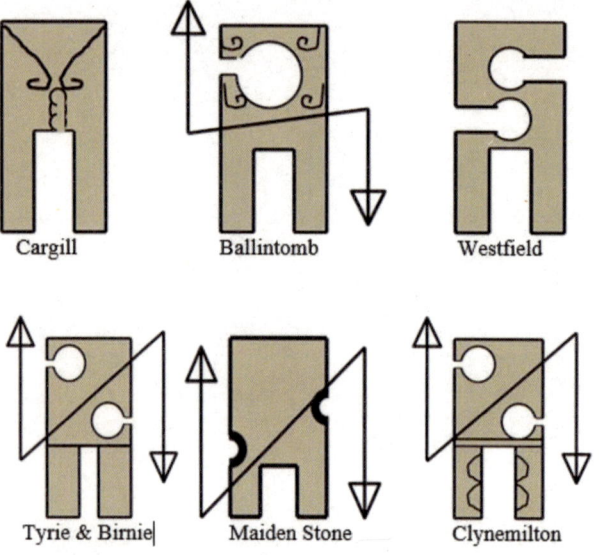